AS GOOD
AS NEW

D0102463

ITV Books

AS GOOD AS NEW

Mike Smith

ITV Books

In association with Yorkshire Television

Editorial: John Doyle, Julie Payne, Eric Smith
Design: Jeremy Dixon

INDEPENDENT TELEVISION BOOKS LTD
247 Tottenham Court Road, London W1P 0AU

First published 1981

© Text, Mike Smith 1981

© As Good As New, Yorkshire Television, a member of
the Trident Television Group, 1981

© Illustrations, ITV Books 1981

ISBN: 0 900727 84 5

Set in 10/11 Times Medium by The Yale Press Ltd

CONDITIONS OF SALE

Illustrations by John Higgins

Printed in Great Britain by Whitstable Litho Ltd,
Millstrood Road, Whitstable, Kent

Contents

Introduction

It is not everyone who finds an interest in old furniture and other items from the past but it is something that seems to grow on a lot of people as they become older and more aware of our history being either thrown away or neglected until it is beyond repair. Being actively involved in antiques I too often learn about items from the past that have been destroyed or carelessly disposed of and nearly everyone you speak to will tell a similar story: "Oh, my granny had one of those and threw it away." There is nothing to be done about the items that are lost except that if any part of the item does remain it can perhaps be used in restoring something that can be saved.

Years ago people threw away items that we now think are valuable. But what are we throwing away and burning today that our future generations will value? Even when we do find an otherwise worthy item of furniture I have seen many disasters caused by people's ignorance. I have found items of polished furniture that have been painted or items that were originally painted, stripped of all their decoration — legs sawn off, backs of dressers cut lower or removed completely, cornices cut to fit into an alcove — the list goes on.

All I ask is that if you find a piece of furniture that you like and it perhaps does not fit into a recess, do not cut off anything to make it fit. Try and sell the item and purchase another one that does fit. If there is no alternative and you cut or remove any part of a piece of furniture do not discard it — put it in a safe place so that if at any time you wish to dispose of the item you will have all the original pieces.

The moral to all this is, if you are not sure about a piece of furniture or any item you wish to restore, ask a qualified antique dealer whether or not you should restore it as any damage incurred by over-zealous work and ignorance can destroy the beauty of the item and devalue it at a stroke. With this most important point in mind do read on and learn how and where to buy old furniture. Go out and find something of our heritage. You will also find that furnishing a home this way is much cheaper and infinitely more fun than buying new factory-made furniture — much of which I cannot see lasting 20 years let alone becoming the antiques of tomorrow.

M.S.1981

Buying

Nearly everyone has a story to tell about auctions – of bargains lost and bargains won. The auction houses are still the main source of supply for all antique dealers and how often have I stood at an auction and heard someone say: 'Oh, antique dealers! They buy everything – I didn't get a chance to buy.' Well, more fool you. Antique dealers do buy a lot from auctions but remember that they will probably have to restore the item they have bought, put it on display in their shop or perhaps wait several weeks before they sell it at a profit. So if there is an item of furniture you wish to buy, bid for it. The antique dealer will probably fall out of the bidding before you, uttering 'Oh, private people buy everything – I didn't have a chance!.'

The biggest single problem about buying at auctions is how much one should pay for an item. As this book deals mainly with Edwardian and Victorian furniture and not with buying or restoring period pieces, we can therefore look at present-day prices of new furniture and use these as our guide.

Let us take as an example an extending dining table that seats six to eight people and is of the type you wind out with a sort of starting handle (Fig 1). This type of table often turns up in auctions, in many cases without the centre leaves. They are usually made of mahogany, oak or walnut and are on brass cup castors. Let us assume that the centre leaves are missing and the general appearance of the table is scruffy, so we must allow for the cost of the new leaves and a repolish.

Now take a trip to your local furnishers and see what price a good-quality new table will cost. I would guess it will be around

£300 for a reproduction of a similar type. Bear in mind that this may well be made of veneer chipboard and have a sprayed-on antique finish. So with this price in mind let us go back to the auction. It may surprise you that tables of this type, in the condition described, can still be bought for around £50–60. Now let us assume that you bought the table and had two leaves made by a professional joiner. This would cost you approximately £40–50. If you then had the table stripped, stained and repolished — matching in the new leaves to the existing table — this would add to the cost a further £60–70, giving a total of £150–180 which represents a great saving against buying new furniture. But if you were able to do the work yourself or even part of it — for example, stripping off all the old polish — the savings are enormous. As a bonus, should you wish to sell your old table you could make a handsome profit, enabling you to make another purchase such as a nicer, older table.

Fig 1 An extending dining table

There would be nothing but gloom, on the other hand, for the person who bought the brand-new table because after perhaps keeping it for two years he will find its resale value only a fraction of the figure that he paid. So the rule is that even if you paid too much money for your item, if you keep it long enough, sometimes only a matter of a few years, it will increase in value to give you a return on your money. You will also have had the pleasure and the use of the item whilst in your home.

The procedure at an auction

So much for the reasons for buying old furniture but let us just go back to the auction because there are some points that are worth going through. There should be no mystique about auctions. They are just places where people take surplus items to sell and other people buy them. If you have never been to an auction before there are certain things to be aware of.

The conditions of the sale   At small local auctions it is as well to ask the auctioneer how payment should be made, what time the auction starts and about the removal of items that have been bought. At larger auctions there will be a catalogue explaining these details. Most auction houses have what is known as a viewing day when you may inspect any of the items for sale. If you intend to bid for an item, it is important to inspect it thoroughly before the start of the auction. If it is a chest of drawers, pull out the drawers and look for wear on the runners. Look at the back for woodworm. Inspect the sides for defects. Check for splits and odd handles, also for handles that are missing or feet that are loose or missing. Look closely at any item you wish to purchase, because at the fall of the hammer the item is yours, faults and all. If there are other items on top of a piece you wish to look at, lift these off or ask a porter to do it for you. It is not unknown for auctioneers to place other items in the sale on or around the item you are interested in so as to cover over a hole, some missing veneer or water stains on a piece of polished furniture. If you do not inspect properly then there is no-one to blame but yourself.

Another point to watch out for is fakes or made-up pieces of furniture, or 'trade pieces' as they are called. If in doubt, ask the opinion of the porters or the auctioneer. They have a certain reputation to keep so they should be able to advise you. The auctioneer or porter will also advise you on what price they think an item will make, thus giving you a guide as to whether or not it is worth bidding for.

Leaving a bid There are several ways of buying at auction. The best way is to go yourself and do your own bidding, but if you are unable to attend the auction you may leave your bid with either the porter or the auctioneer. If you leave your bid with the porter you must write down clearly the lot number and the price you will pay up to. It is customary to tip the porter according to the price of the item but this is at your discretion. Often a porter will have several bids for one item and in this case the following procedure is adopted: Mr Smith left a bid of £30, Mr Jones left £28 and Mr White left £35. If the item was knocked down for, say, £25 then Mr White would be the purchaser as he left the highest bid. He would possibly give a tip of £2 to the porter. If a bid is left with the auctioneer he will write it down on his lot sheet, so when he reaches this number during the auction, he knows he has a bid of, say, £40. Some unscrupulous auctioneers, though in all fairness there are very few, may start the bidding at £40 and if there is no other bid it will be knocked down to you for £40, whereas, if you had attended the auction and started the bidding at, say, £20 you may have bought the item for less than the £40 bid you left with the auctioneer.

Bidding in person It is better, as I have already mentioned, to attend the auction yourself and do your own bidding. If you do, however, it is essential not to get carried away in your bidding. Too often I have seen two parties bidding furiously against each other and one of them finishing up by paying far too much for an item. Armed with a piece of paper with the lot numbers you intend to bid for, plus the price you are willing to go up to, you are now ready for the auction.

When the lot number you are interested in comes up, make your first bid clear to the auctioneer. Make sure he has seen you. After your first bid you can use either a nod, wink, wave, pen, piece of paper or whatever you like to signify that you are still in the bidding. Once the auctioneer knows you are bidding he will keep coming back to you until you stop, usually with a shake of the head. If your bid is successful the auctioneer will ask your name and this will be entered on his sheet. You should also note the lot number and price paid on your paper so as to check the bill when paying for your items at the end of the sale.

Tricks to use when bidding   Tricks sometimes work to get you an item cheaper than your proposed maximum bid. When the lot you wish to buy comes up, for example, do not bid at the beginning but wait until there are only two bidders left. Just before the hammer is about to drop, put up your hand quickly and call out 'Yes', 'Here', or something similar. The auctioneer then usually calls out 'New bid' and since the previous bidder is caught off guard, you can sometimes have the item knocked down to you before he wakes up.

Bidding often starts low. I have often seen articles knocked down for £200 where the bidding has started at £5. The reason for this is that someone thinks he is in for a bargain. Equally, I have found that by starting the bidding high often startles other intending bidders and before they can nod, the item has been knocked down.

Let us say, for example, an item is going to fetch around £150. Bidding would normally start around £40–50 and work its way up to the estimated selling price. The auctioneer's patter would be roughly as follows: 'What may I say? £80? [pause] £70? [pause] Well, someone start me off at £50.' At this point call out '£110'. Whilst everyone is looking for you, you could have the item knocked down to you for the maiden bid, as it is called.

Another way of bidding is to bid as though you are going to have the item at any cost, by exaggerating your bids with your hand or by calling out 'Yes' on your bid. Often this will put other people off. Also just by keeping your hand in the air will sometimes put off other bidders. You may, of course, have your own method of bidding. It is all a game and great fun at auctions trying to outdo and outbid your competitors, and it is interesting to watch other people bid. Learn by their mistakes. Watch and learn the good points and tricks that other people use. These methods of bidding do not work all the time, but it gives pleasure to you when they do.

Replacing materials

Do not forget that when you restore old furniture you will often have to replace broken or wormy wood, so auctions are good hunting grounds for materials such as wood, hinges and handles. Many old wardrobes are made of solid walnut, mahogany or oak and can be bought for just a few pounds but one that is broken and beyond repair will give up a wealth of materials. The sides of a mahogany wardrobe would make the two leaves for the table we spoke about earlier and leave plenty of other timber for repairs. You could also gain brass handles, locks, hinges — perhaps even a full-length mirror. So bear in mind this type of furniture, especially as new wood is so expensive nowadays and tends to be inferior to the old woods. Remember also that the old wood will be thoroughly dry and less likely to twist or warp.

Other likely sources of old furniture

Auctions are probably the best place for buying old furniture but there are many other sources for picking up the odd piece. Have a good look at the bench or toolbox in your garden shed — the most incredible items come from sources such as this. Items are often in poor condition but save them if you can. I hate to see what was good furniture go beyond hope of repair simply through neglect and ignorance of what it once was.

Newspaper advertisements are worth looking through as quite often a bargain appears. You will have to be quick though because you are not the only prospective buyer. Post office windows with their array of postcards advertising prams, cycles, lawnmowers, etc, are worth keeping an eye on. Occasionally in the middle of all these you may find 'Old mahogany chest of drawers — needs repair. £5. You should have a look at it because the handles alone could be worth double the asking price.

Then there is a variety of shops — antique, second-hand, charity, etc. There are bargains to be had in many of the smaller antique shops. I have had some of my best buys in antique shops, ranging from furniture to china. When buying from antique shops ask the proprietor if he or she has any old furniture that he does not wish to repair himself and which he may be willing to sell. Most antique shops have something they wish to sell because they lack the time in which to restore it or the space is required for some other item. Often if it has been in the dealer's way for a long time the price could be quite favourable.

Because an item of furniture is in an antique shop it does not mean that it will necessarily be expensive. Many antique dealers only buy from other shops and it is quite common to be able to trace a piece of furniture around a city as it goes from one shop to another, inevitably getting more expensive every time it changes hands. This happens time after time because, for example, a small

16

shop on the outskirts of a town will not have the same clientele nor such large overheads as that of a sizeable shop in the centre of town. This means that the shop on the outskirts would sell an item for, say, £100 but the same article transferred to the town-centre shop would be priced at about £175. So there are always bargains to be had if you happen to be in the right place at the right time.

Tools
and Adhesives

You may already have a basic tool-kit but there are a number of rather specialised tools that are required in the restoration of old furniture. They are not cheap nowadays so they need to be looked after and well maintained; they will then give you a lifetime of service. Whilst searching for pieces of furniture you may come across old and second-hand tools that can be cleaned and restored themselves. In fact, many old tools are better made than their modern counterparts. Remember that a new plane iron can be purchased if the old one is worn out, but do not throw away the old one as this will make an ideal scraper for removing old paint and varnish.

Tools that you may need

Let us look at some of the tools you may use in the course of restoring a piece of furniture.

Screwdrivers Three different-size screwdrivers — small, medium and large — will remove most screws.

Saws A small-to-medium tenon saw and a panel saw will be sufficient for all straight cuts, but many jobs on old furniture will require curves so a coping saw will be a useful addition to your tool-kit. These little saws are quite inexpensive and will do most jobs requiring curved cuts up to 5cm (2in) thick if you are patient and do not put excessive pressure on the blade.

Fig 1 Saws and hammers

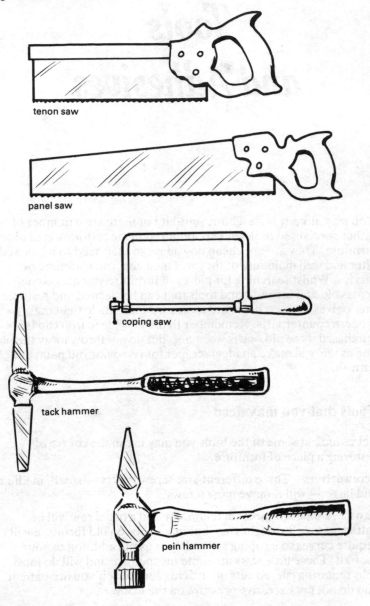

tenon saw

panel saw

coping saw

tack hammer

pein hammer

Hammers Every home has a hammer of some sort. The most useful type is the pein hammer. Select one weighing about 280 g (10 oz) which will do most jobs, although you may find a use for ball pein and claw hammers. If you wish to tackle upholstery it would be useful to have an upholstery tack hammer which has a magnetic end on the head which will pick up tacks and save you from pricking your fingers trying to pick them up yourself.

Chisels These are a most important part of any tool-kit but, more than any other tool, they are useless and dangerous unless they are kept sharp. The maintenance and sharpening of tools will be described and dealt with later. Three chisels will do most jobs, although you may find that you require a full set. Start off with bevel-edge chisels of these sizes: 6 mm (¼ in), 12 mm (½ in), 18 mm (¾ in) and 25 mm (1 in).

Planes These are perhaps the most expensive items to buy but they form a most important part of the equipment. First you will need a 5 cm (2 in) *smoothing plane* for general woodwork and for the removal of large amounts of wood. The next requirement is a *block plane* which is used for fine work because of the low angle of the blade. This type can be used for planing the edges of veneer and even across the grain of wood. When set very fine the thinnest of shavings can be removed. Always, on any plane, try the blade setting on a piece of scrap wood first as it is very disappointing, because of an incorrect setting, to find you have chipped off a piece of wood that you have patiently glued and fitted. Also needed is a *shoulder plane* — a very accurate type — used by all joiners and one that I use as much as any plane on very fine work. As the blade cuts right into an edge it is very useful for replacing stringing (decorative hardwood edges), planing the edge of veneers and getting right into awkward corners.

With these three planes in your tool-kit you will be able to accomplish most of the jobs in restoring furniture. There are, of course, many other planes you could add to your tool-kit. Three later additions I would recommend are as follows. Similar to a shoulder plane, a *bullnose plane* will allow you to remove wood right up to an edge as the blade is only 3 mm (⅛ in) from the front of the plane. A *steel jack plane* is used for jointing two lengths of timber together. Due to the jack plane's longer overall length it is easier to use when planing a long length of timber to fit. The third type is a *spokeshave*. As the name implies this tool was originally used to fashion spokes for cartwheels. It is useful for any curved work and comes in a variety of different sizes. Your first purchase should be one with a curved bottom as this will plane concave, convex and flat surfaces.

Fig 2 Planes

smoothing plane

block plane

shoulder plane

spokeshave

Fig 3 Other necessary tools

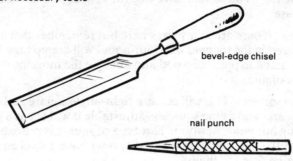

bevel-edge chisel

nail punch

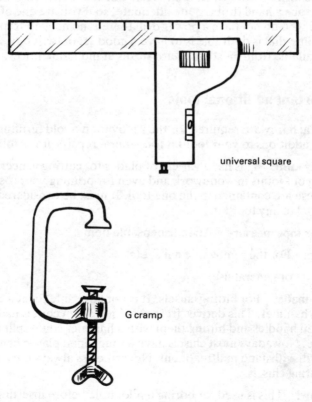

universal square

G cramp

Nail punches   You should have one for veneer pins and one for general use.

G cramps   There are many sizes here but remember that a piece of cord used in the manner of a tourniquet will cramp together many a chair and piece of wood and must be the most inexpensive cramp available.

Universal square   This will act as a right-angle square and 45° mitre square, and as the square is adjustable it will act as a gauge for setting out joints in wood. This type of square is probably the most useful of all tools as good quality ones have a level and a metal scribe fitted to them.

Drills   The restoration of old furniture will very often involve the use of a drill — whether it be an electric drill or a hand drill. In my experience a hand drill is quite adequate, so if you are one of those people who do not have a power drill there is no need to fret. The only thing that is desirable is to have a good set of twist bits. These are available from most hardware stores at moderate prices.

Important additional tools

General hardware required for the renovation of old furniture and useful additions to your tool-kit for general repairs are as follows.

Stanley knife   This has a variety of blades for cutting veneers, setting out joints in woodwork and even for pruning your roses. All these are contained in the one tool. It must be considered an essential to any tool-kit.

Rule or tape measure   An indispensable item.

Pincers   For the removal of nails, etc.

Pliers   For general use.

Wood mallet   For hitting chisels. It is not advisable to hit a chisel with a hammer. This derives from the times when chisels had wooden handles and hitting them with a hammer could split the handle. Nowadays most chisels have a toughened plastic handle that will withstand maltreatment. Nevertheless always use a mallet for hitting chisels.

Bradawl   This is used for boring a pilot hole before inserting a

Fig 4 Important additional tools

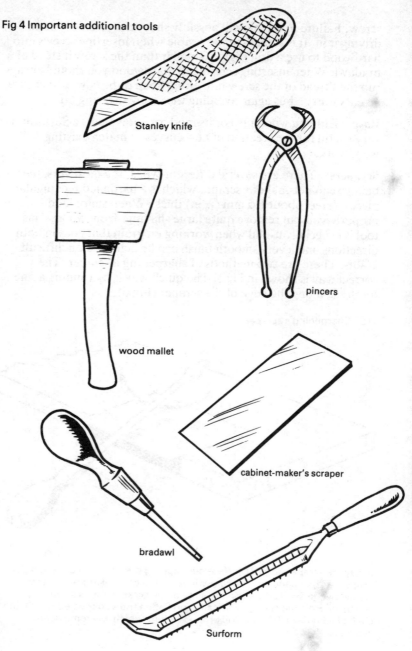

Stanley knife

pincers

wood mallet

cabinet-maker's scraper

bradawl

Surform

screw. Failure to do this will possibly sheer the screw off when driving it in. It is sometimes advisable when inserting screws into hardwood to use a drill slightly smaller than the screw instead of a bradawl. When inserting screws into hardwood you should always rub the thread of the screw into either soap or bees-wax to ensure an easy entry, thus again avoiding the screw sheering off.

Rasp Either a wood rasp or its modern equivalent, a Surform, is very useful for the creation of new curves to match existing woodwork.

Scrapers   There are several different types, the most versatile being a cabinet-maker's scraper which is a hardened rectangular piece of steel about 1½ mm ($\frac{1}{16}$ in) thick. When sharpened properly you can remove quite large shavings from wood. This tool is especially useful when working on grain that goes in both directions and a very smooth finish can be achieved on difficult grains. There are two methods of sharpening a scraper. The correct way is shown in Fig 5. The quick way is by running a fine tooth file along the edge of the scraper (Fig 6).

Fig 5 Sharpening a scraper

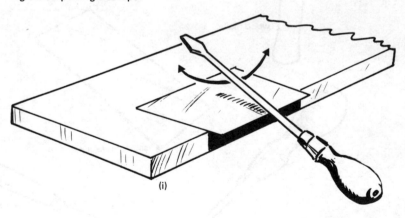

(i)

(i) Lay the scraper on a flat surface overlapping the edge. Hold the scraper firmly with one hand and the screwdriver in the other. The shaft of the screwdriver is worked against the edge of the scraper with a stropping action. (ii) Hold the scraper vertically and flatten the stropped edge with the shaft of a bradawl. (iii) This will produce a burr which will remove fine shavings of wood.

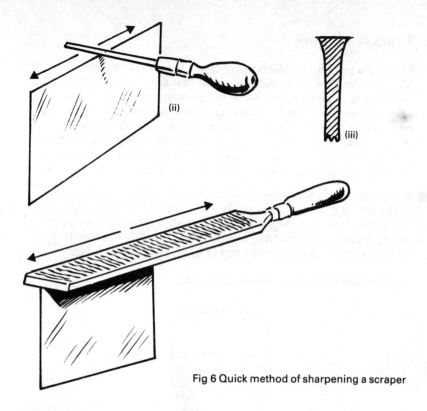

Fig 6 Quick method of sharpening a scraper

Sharpening tools

You will need an oilstone, preferably one that is two-sided. That is to say, one half of the stone is coarse and the other side is fine. Use the coarse side for sharpening tools that have been used on hard and gritty woods, finishing off on the smooth side to achieve a fine cutting edge.

General maintenance

It makes good sense to look after your tools, so every time you finish using them wipe all metal parts with an oily rag to prevent rust. Clean out all old shavings from the mouths of planes and remember to put all tools out of the reach of very small children.

Types of adhesive

There are now many different types of glue on the market.
Manufacturers of many of them claim that they will stick virtually
anything to everything but be wary. So many times I have had to
unglue something that someone has stuck together with the wrong
type. Removing these glues is a tedious job and you can never
make as good a job when gluing for the second time. The types of
glue that I use are both modern and old. Each has its own purpose
and if used correctly should give you no problems.

Animal glue   This type, sometimes known as Scotch glue, is one
of the oldest glues still used today and many restorers prefer it to
any other. Its only failing is that it is not waterproof but it can be
used for general woodwork, joints, splicing and veneering. It does,
however, need special equipment (Fig 7). Half fill the larger

Fig 7 Special equipment for heating animal glue

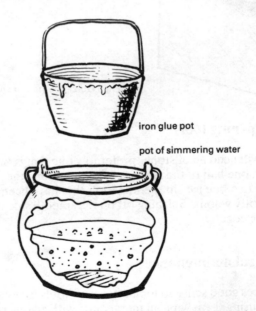

iron glue pot

pot of simmering water

container with water then add the dry pellets to the top container
and just cover them with water. Put the top container into the
bottom one, place on a gas ring and bring the water to the boil.

Once the water has reached boiling point turn down the heat until the water simmers. In time the glue pellets will melt. More water can be added to the glue to give the right consistency for the job in hand. Never let the water container boil dry. Top up with water when necessary. Stir the mixture until the water and pellets look like a runny treacle. The glue is then ready to be applied using an old 18 mm (¾ in) paintbrush.

PVA   The white woodworker's glue, this is good for all clean wood joints but not so good on old broken joints unless all traces of old glue are removed. This type of glue, like animal glue, is not waterproof.

Cascomite   A powder glue good for most woodwork, this is also a good gap filler, so it is ideal for a loose joint. To mix you just add water to the powder making it to the consistency you require. This glue is waterproof.

Epoxy resin two pack   This usually comes in two small tubes and is ideal for woodwork joints, china repairs, metal, stone, etc. Its main use is on smaller jobs as it is quite expensive.

Copydex   This is a latex rubber based glue that is ideal for fabrics or gluing down leathers on writing tables and boxes.

Contact adhesive   This type always seems to be used in the wrong place. Veneer can be stuck down quite successfully with it, also leather and flexible materials can be stuck to wood forming a very strong bond but do not use this type for sticking the legs of chairs etc.

Repairs to Wood

There are so many different types of repair when restoring old furniture that it is impossible to describe them all. Many will be of a type where only your own ingenuity will be able to effect the repair. However, some types of repair crop up again and again and these follow a similar procedure with, of course, variations.

Chairs

Loose joints   Both old and new chairs tend to work loose and considering the amount of wear and tear they go through in the normal day it is not surprising. Loose joints are fairly easy to repair if the chair is not the upholstered type.

Let us take, for example, an all-wood chair with loose legs. Carefully knock apart all the joints with a wooden mallet, so as not to bruise the wood. As each leg comes free, pencil a number both on the leg and next to the corresponding hole it was removed from. Do the same with the under-braces (Fig 1). Clean off any old glue from the joints.

Using a PVA glue apply and fit the chair stretcher together. Do not fit the pieces tightly yet. Glue each of the legs and insert them into the corresponding holes. It may be helpful if you have some assistance when fitting the stretcher into the chair legs as it is quite a struggle trying to fit four joints into wobbly legs.

When the stretcher has been inserted into the legs gently tap the joints home. Place the chair, legs up, on a table or bench and knock the legs firmly home into the seat joints. Place a double

Fig 1 First stage in repairing loose joints

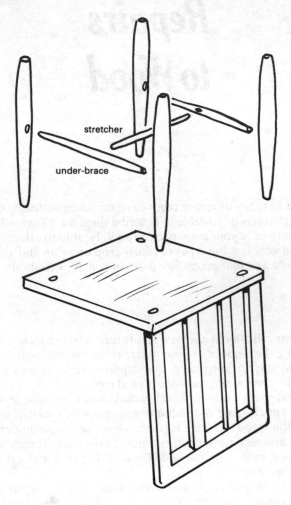

stretcher

under-brace

length of rope, say, sash cord, round the chair legs (Fig 2) and with a scrap piece of wood wind up the rope like a tourniquet. Protect the legs of the chair where the rope is liable to bruise the edges. A piece of thick cardboard will do this job quite adequately. Leave the glue to set before removing the tourniquet and leave the chair a further eight hours before putting it back into use.

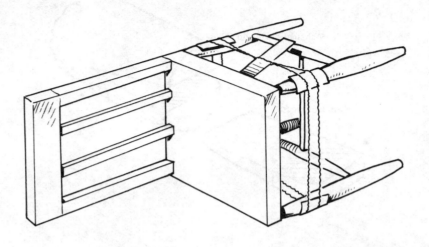

Wedging a chair leg   If a chair leg is too loose in the joint then the method for securing the leg is this. First cut a V-shaped slot in the end of the leg (Fig 3). Then cut a hardwood wedge slightly larger than the V slot you have made. Apply glue to the wedge and to the end of the leg. Place the wedge in the V slot. As the leg is driven home into the chair socket the wedge will expand the leg thus giving a good strong join when the glue has set.

There are some important tips that will assist you when carrying out this type of repair.

1   Wipe off any glue that seeps out of the joins. Do this with a damp cloth.

2   After having glued the legs and applied the tourniquet stand the chair on a level, flat surface to ensure that the chair is level as the glue dries.

3   Putting screws or, worse still, nails into loose or wobbly chairs is a waste of time as after a few weeks of normal use the chair will start to wobble again. It then becomes a problem to remove the nails and screws and after this is done it will leave unsightly holes.

4   Metal angle brackets are often used for strengthening chairs. These must be considered only as a temporary measure as these too will work loose in time.

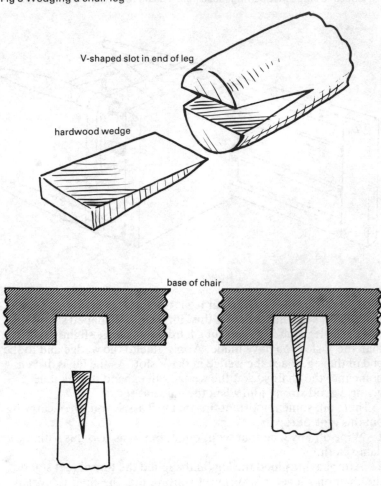

Fig 3 Wedging a chair leg

V-shaped slot in end of leg

hardwood wedge

base of chair

Broken joints There are two main types of joints in chairs. The mortise and tenon joint is generally found in most older types of chairs and furniture. Later furniture manufacturers used, and still use, the other type — the dowel joint (Fig 4). If a dowel joint is broken it is not too difficult to repair. Cut the broken dowel level with the shoulder of the piece of wood and drill out the stump with a twist drill of the same size. Once this is drilled out replace the

Fig 4 Common joints in chairs

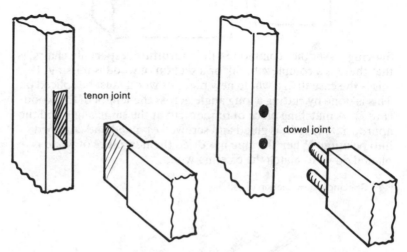

dowel with a new one, making sure the length will fit into both holes. Failure to check this will result in the shoulders not coming together. A small slot made with a tenon saw along the length of the dowel will allow the glue to squeeze out and the joint will fit more snugly (Fig 5).

Fig 5 Slot cut into dowel to let out excess glue

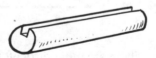

Tenons that are broken are somewhat more difficult to repair and you will have to fit a whole new section into the rail (Fig 6). Do make sure you take accurate measurements or a pattern of the old rail and tenon. If the complete rail has broken or is beyond repair then take a pattern from the other rail on the opposite side of the chair.

Fig 6 Fitting a new tenon

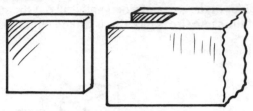

Splicing   Another common fault in furniture, especially chairs, is that there is a complete break or a section of wood is missing. If this is the case then a whole new piece of wood must be spliced on. This is done by cutting a long angle across the length of the wood (Fig 7). A matching piece of timber, cut at the same angle and the appropriate length, is glued and screwed or glued and cramped into position. When the glue has dried the new piece of wood is planed down to match the existing wood.

Fig 7 Splicing a new section of rail

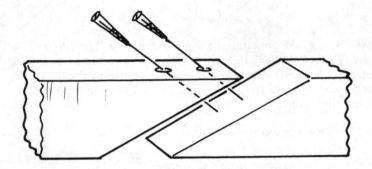

Upholstered chairs   These are more difficult to repair because of the fabric covering and webbing. This is fine if the chair is to be re-upholstered because the old material, stuffing and webbing can be removed before starting any repairs to the joints or legs. Should you not wish to strip the chair completely, you will have to take great care not to disturb the stuffing and webbing on the chair. It is advisable, though, to remove the top cover to allow you to make the repairs to any of the joints. It will also avoid staining the cover with any surplus glue. When the chair has been repaired and the glue dry the outer cover can be replaced.

Drawers

In the league table of repairs probably the next most common is those to drawers. Think how many times a drawer is opened and shut; over a number of years this causes wear to the runners of the drawers and to the drawer itself.

Sticking and stiff drawers If a drawer is sticking the remedy is to rub the runners of the drawer and its sides with either a wax candle or a piece of soap. After this treatment you will find the drawer

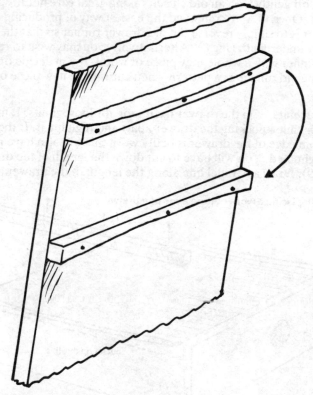

Fig 8 Reversing a worn drawer runner in a chest of drawers

will glide in and out easily. Should the drawer be very stiff you may have to plane a thin shaving from either the side or top and bottom of the drawer. Do not overdo this or you will find the drawer will be very sloppy and this will very quickly cause wear on the runners.

Worn runners   You may have noticed that some drawers seem to tip when you shut them. This is usually caused by excessive wear on the drawer runners on the side of the chest of drawers. Remove the drawer and look at the runners on the carcass. If they are badly worn they will need to be replaced. These runners may be either screwed or just glued to the sides of the carcass. If they are screwed then it is a simple job just to release the screws to remove the runners. If the runners are glued on, you will have to prise them off gently with an old chisel, taking great care not to split the wood. Once they are removed the easiest way of producing a new runner is to simply reverse the old drawer runner so that the worn side is underneath (Fig 8). Alternatively, you may wish to replace the runner with a whole new piece of wood. If you decide on this, use the old runner as a pattern when cutting the new piece of wood.

Loose joints   On the drawer itself look for loose joints. It may be worthwhile knocking the drawer apart and regluing it. If the bottom edge of the drawer is badly worn this will also have to be straightened. You will have to cut down the length of the drawer (Fig 9). Draw a parallel line along the length of the drawer and cut

Fig 9 Replacing a worn bottom edge of a drawer

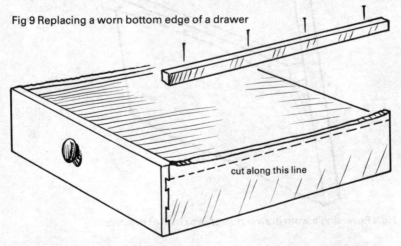

cut along this line

along this line very carefully. After the section of wood has been removed, plane off the rough saw edge and glue and nail in a new piece of wood cut to the size of the piece you have removed. Remember to punch in the nails, for any nail that protrudes will cut into the wood runners on the carcass, causing the drawer to grate and wear out very quickly.

Shrinkage The bottom of drawers tend to shrink away from the front edge. To remedy this, remove the nails or screws from the back of the drawer (Fig 10). After these have been removed the drawer bottom may be tapped up with a mallet so that it fits into the groove on the front of the drawer. Replace the screws or nails to hold the bottom in place. You will not be able to use the same holes, so if screws are used you will have to bore new holes so the screws fit into the back of the drawer.

Fig 10 Remedying shrinkage

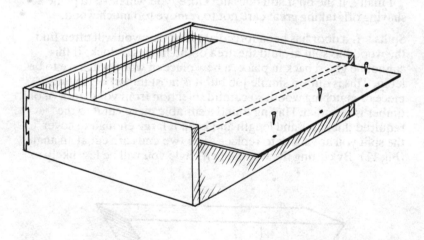

Doors

The biggest problem with doors is that often they do not shut properly. Before you reach for your plane try and find the cause.

Hinges Usually the fault is with the hinges. Either they are badly worn or loose. Often over the years the screws holding the hinges become loose in the wood. Try and tighten the screws. If they spin round in the wood without pulling the hinge tight you will have to remove the door and plug the screw hole with a thin piece of wood glued into place. Often a matchstick will do this job. When the glue has dried fit back the door using a bradawl to allow easier starting of the screw.

It is quite acceptable to pack out the hinges to make a door fit. This is done by putting cardboard under the hinges before tightening up the screws. This will also stop the door becoming hinge-bound. This is quite a common fault which occurs when the hinge has been let into the wood too far and will not allow easy closing of the door. If the problem remains after adjusting the hinges, check that the screw heads in the hinges are not protruding above the countersunk part of the hinge. If this is the fault then you will either have to replace the screws with smaller heads or remove the screws and countersink the hinges a little deeper.

Finally, if the door still does not close, you will have to plane a shaving off, taking great care not to remove too much wood.

Splits If a door has been forced at some time you will often find the wood has split around the area of the hinges or lock. If this cannot be glued back in place, a new piece of wood will have to be let in. This is quite a simple job but it is most important to find a piece of matching wood, so careful selection from your stock of old timber is essential. Having found a suitable piece cut it to the required thickness and length and keep it large enough to cover the split you are about to replace. The two ends are cut at an angle (Fig 11). By cutting the wood on an angle you will be less likely to

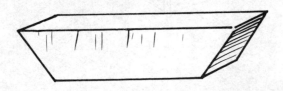

Fig 11 Piece of wood cut to replace a split section

notice the join. Square cuts show up very badly when the finished job is polished. Using the shaped piece as a pattern, score a line with a sharp modeller's knife around the edges of the piece of wood you are going to cut out from the carcass (Fig 12). It may

Fig 12 Scoring the shape of replacement piece

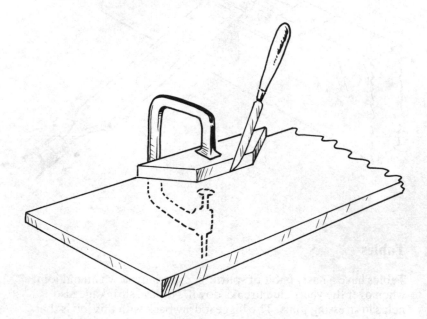

help you to hold the new piece of wood down with a cramp whilst marking out. Using a tenon saw, cut down the two angled lines, then cut a series of straight cuts down to the other scribed line. Using a very sharp 25 mm (1 in) chisel pare out the pieces of wood, down to the scribed line (Fig 13). Make sure the final cuts leave the wood square and true. You should find the new piece of wood will fit properly. Once the piece of wood has been fitted, apply a film of PVA glue to the two surfaces and cramp into position. When the glue has dried the new piece of wood can be planed down to the level of the surrounding wood, then stained and polished to match.

Fig 13 Chiselling away damaged section

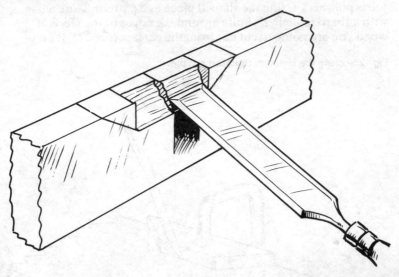

Tables

Tables have a nasty habit of splitting, especially down an old join,
when over the years glue breaks down. Natural shrinkage also
helps in stressing joins. The biggest drawback with this job is that
it is almost certain that the table top will need to be repolished as
you will never, except on very rare occasions, manage to join the
two pieces back dead level so the top will have to be sanded or
planed level.

Jointing leaves   When jointing two table leaves you must first
remove all traces of the old glue with a scraper. Then place the two
leaves together and see if they fit close all the way along the edge.
If there is a small gap anywhere along the length you must use a
plane to smooth down any bumps. When jointing long lengths
together it is better to use a steel jack plane as this will help you to
achieve a straight edge. Make sure also that the joint is square
otherwise when you come to glue the two pieces together the table
will not be flat.

When you feel the two edges are perfectly straight and square fit them together to make sure there are no gaps and the two table pieces are perfectly flat. Apply PVA glue to the two pieces and cramp together. Sash cramps will be needed for this operation. If you do not have any you can hire them for a nominal sum from a local hire company. It is possible to cramp them together by the use of wedges (Fig 14), but first lay sheets of newspaper under the

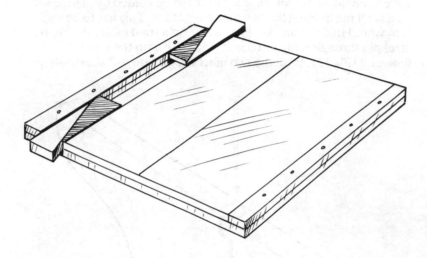

Fig 14 Wedging table leaves together after gluing

join where the glue is liable to squeeze out. The excess glue can be scraped off after it has dried. Remove any surplus glue from the top with a damp cloth and make sure the edges on the top of the table are as flush as possible. You must try and avoid one being higher than the other as this will give you more work when it comes to sanding the two surfaces level before polishing.

Replacing swing brackets It has always amazed me that tables, often small ones with drop leaves, are normally only affected by woodworm on one part — usually the swing brackets that hold up the leaves. I can understand them being worn because of use over the years, but why the woodworm specialises in eating these brackets I shall never know.

Replacing these brackets is a job that is not too difficult because they are usually screwed on and can be easily removed. Once they have been taken off you have a pattern to be guided by. There will be a steel pin holding the two pieces together. This has to be removed. Hold the bracket in a vice or on a solid table. Punch the steel pin through using a 100 mm (4 in) nail with the point flattened (Fig 15). With the two pieces apart you will see the shape

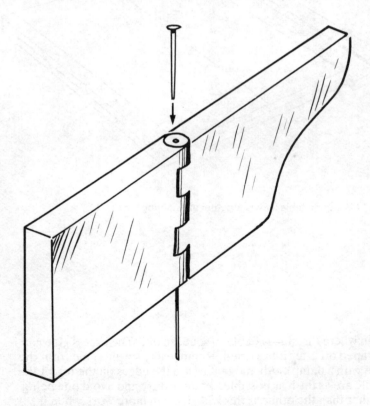

Fig 15 Removing steel hinge pin from swing bracket

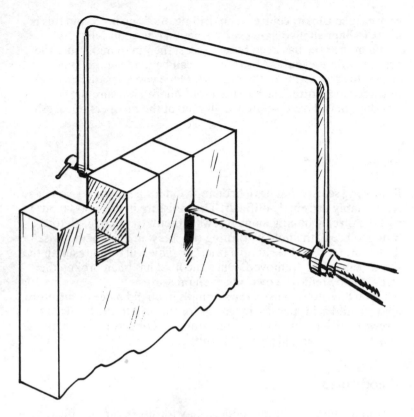

Fig 16 Removing pieces of wood with coping saw

of the fingers and sockets and how these must be cut. Select a compatible piece of wood and cut and plane it to the same width and thickness as the bracket you have removed. Set out on the new piece the identical pattern using a modeller's knife. Cut down the vertical lines using a tenon saw. A coping saw is used for removing the piece of wood (Fig 16). Trim the rough edges with a sharp chisel.

The hole for the pin must be bored using a hand drill the same size as the pin. Mark the centre of the hole and holding the drill perfectly upright drill the hole. You will find it easier to drill from the top and the bottom so that the holes meet in the middle. It is very easy to run off centre when drilling one long hole, and this is likely to happen if you are even a fraction out of upright.

When the hole has been bored, insert the pin to make sure the bracket swings evenly. Adjustments can be made at this stage to ensure the free swing of the bracket. Once you are satisfied, the bracket can be fitted back to the table where I am sure the woodworm will be absolutely delighted at the prospect of a fresh meal.

Screws

Removing screws that have been in wood for a hundred years or so is invariably extremely difficult. The moisture in the wood tends to rust the thread making many screws difficult to remove. Before trying to break the hold by turning the screw in an anticlockwise direction, try to tighten it up a fraction. This will often result in the screw being easily removed. Once the hold has been broken the screw can be removed by using even pressure.

If you have to replace screws or nails in an old piece of furniture, apply a mild acid such as vinegar or formic acid to the heads of the screws to give them an older appearance. New screws and nails look terrible in an old piece of furniture.

Woodworm

All old furniture and even modern-day furniture can be affected by this little pest. It is as well to know a little bit about the life-cycle of the woodworm.

It lives for about three years, laying its eggs in crevices in wood during spring and early summer. As the grubs hatch, they bore their way into the wood and remain concealed for about two years. Later on they change into winged beetles gnawing their way to the surface leaving tiny round holes and fine powdered dust. The winged beetles then mate immediately and lay their eggs in any small crevice thus starting the whole cycle over again.

As these beetles can fly, almost any piece of furniture can be affected with the possible exception of solid mahogany and teak. Nevertheless, woodworm can be killed quite easily so do not despair if you find signs of them in your furniture.

If the affected wood is hollow and soft to the touch then that section will have to be replaced. If there are only a few holes and the wood feels quite sound, then you may inject the holes with one of the commercial insecticides. Some of these are available with a long spout for inserting into the holes and a good squeeze will penetrate, killing all the grubs. The most successful method I have found is by using a large plastic hypodermic syringe with a fine needle attached. After filling the syringe put the needle into the hole and give a good squirt until the hole will take no more liquid. Each hole must be treated to ensure that all the grubs are killed. Rubbing over the surface of the wood with rag charged with insecticide will not be enough. Be careful of marking the finished surfaces as some insecticides will stain. Wipe off any surplus immediately with a clean cloth.

Splits and shakes

Apart from finding pieces missing or broken on a piece of furniture, you may find structural repairs are needed. Over the years wood tends to shrink as the moisture dries out. This causes defects such as shakes and knots that fall out. Warping is another serious problem on large flat surfaces of wood.

Warped wood and shakes are often caused by standing a piece of furniture near a radiator or even if it is kept in a room where there is not enough moisture. The simple answer to this is to keep the furniture away from any direct heat and try to keep the room well ventilated. If the room is closed then place a decorative bowl next to the heat source and fill this with water. This will need to be kept topped up with water and you will be surprised how much of this water will evaporate. Commercial humidifiers are available, some of which hang on the radiator. The choice is yours: a little inconvenience of the bowls of water or ruined furniture. Do not forget that the sun shining through a window will create a lot of heat and will also bleach any wood that is in direct light very quickly.

Fillers

When making repairs to any wood it is sometimes more suitable to fill in defects with a filler rather than let in a new piece of wood.

This may be frowned upon by some professionals but letting in new pieces of wood often involves disturbing the polish of the surrounding area; in addition, the new piece will have to be stained and polished to match. So on small defects I feel that fillers can be used quite effectively, but I do not advocate that they should be used excessively.

Shellac Small shakes can be filled with a shellac filler. These can be bought from polish suppliers in a whole range of different colours, enabling you to match any wood; they can also be intermixed. You can, of course, make your own coloured filler by melting the shellac and adding powdered wood dyes. The shakes or holes are filled by heating the blade of an old knife which is then put on to the end of shellac stick so that the melted shellac drips into the split. Using the still warm knife smooth the shellac level with the surface of the surrounding wood.

Bees-wax As well as making superb wax polish, bees-wax will make a good filler for smaller holes, such as nail holes and woodworm holes, if a wood dye is added to it. Add the required amount of dye to the melted bees-wax and stir until the dye is thoroughly mixed in. Put the mixture aside to set and when it is hard it can be used for filling any small hole. It is best applied with an old kitchen knife or putty knife, smoothing off with a sanding block wrapped in a piece of old rag. This not only fills in the holes but produces a beautiful shine as well. Powdered resin can be added to this filler. This will make the bees-wax slightly harder and thus more suitable for larger holes.

I have mentioned that bees-wax makes very good furniture polish – it is probably the oldest polish in the world. The method I use to make the polish is as follows. First, melt 200 g (½ lb) of pure bees-wax. Care must be taken here as too much heat will cause the wax to ignite. Treat the melting of the wax as if you were heating up lard or oil for cooking chips. When the wax has melted remove it from the heat and add to it ½ litre (1 pint) of turpentine substitute. Some people prefer to use pure turpentine. Stir the mixture very thoroughly and put it to one side to set. When the wax has set it is ready for use. By using bees-wax over a period of time your furniture will take on a superb patina, or sheen. Wax polish requires elbow grease when it is being applied to the wood but your efforts will be rewarded.

Never apply silicon-based polishes to wood. These, in time, will cause a bloom to appear. The worst offenders in this respect are aerosol sprays; although they are very convenient for use on glass and ceramic tiles, they will cause untold trouble after continued use on wood.

Stripping Furniture

Several years ago it was very fashionable to buy old furniture, such as polished chairs, chests of drawers and cupboards and paint them to match existing colour schemes around the home. But times change. Now everyone is removing all the paint in order to restore the furniture to its former glory, which I might add I am very pleased to see.

There are certain types of furniture, however, which should not be stripped. Some old furniture was intended to be painted and skilfully decorated and once stripped this type of furniture could not be restored to its original condition. It is vital that if you suspect that a piece of furniture might be of value, you should consult an expert before taking an irrevocable step.

Equally the same is true of some Victorian and Edwardian furniture. Pine or softwoods were used for cheaper items of furniture rather than the more popular mahogany and walnut, but the softwoods were used with great skill. Tradesmen from these periods would grain the wood to make it look like the more expensive hardwoods. It is as well at this point to explain the procedure for graining taking, for example, a chest of drawers.

Graining wood

The whole carcass would be made in softwood and this would be sanded down until it was smooth. Any knot holes would be cut out and new wood fitted in their place. The same would apply with any other defects. (Quite often when stripping off old paint, you will find the wood underneath looking like a patchwork quilt.) When all the defects were filled and the chest fully sanded, the next process was to apply a thin layer of plaster, which in turn was again sanded smooth. This gave a very good surface for the next job, which was the actual graining.

Coloured pigments were often added to the plaster to give a good base colour for the graining. For example, when a mahogany finish was required a red pigment was used with the plaster and today when stripping pine or softwoods you will often find this pigment the most difficult to remove. This is because the red pigment penetrated deeply into the bare wood when the plaster was applied. After the plaster coat had dried this was, as I have mentioned, then sanded smooth and the skilled art of the grainer began.

The grainer used a number of items in his work such as combs, sponges, turkey feathers, brushes and rags. These highly skilled tradesmen would transform ordinary wood into figured mahogany, rosewood, walnut, oak, etc. There are many examples of this type of work in various museums around the country and, time permitting, you really ought to look at them. You will realise the great skill that went into producing this type of finish. When the graining had been completed and left to dry, a final coat of polish was applied to protect the grained surface.

It seems hard to believe now that all this work and skill went into a plain softwood chest in order to produce an item of furniture which would look like its solid hardwood counterpart at a fraction of the cost. It does seem a great shame that this art has almost been lost and is now only practised by a small number of people.

So the moral of this is, if the item of furniture is in its original grained finish and in fair condition, it would look much better if it was left as it was.

How to strip a piece of furniture

Finding cheap furniture is getting more difficult as stripping furniture has become popular over recent years. In many homes, however, old cupboards and chests of drawers have been used in garden sheds and garages to store all manner of things. When stripped, renovated and repolished these look splendid in the home.

Preparation First protect the floor because any solvents dripping onto the floor will either remove the polish or mark the surface. The floor should be covered with an old sheet of hardboard or something similar. Tools required for removing paint are a stiff bristle brush, toothbrush, wire brush, cabinet scraper, painter's broadknife, metal bucket, wire wool, paint scrapers and paint kettle (or tin) for the stripping agent (Fig 1).

Fig 1 Tools for stripping furniture

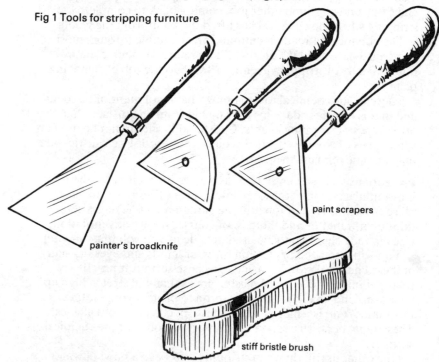

paint scrapers

painter's broadknife

stiff bristle brush

Paint removers There are many types on the market and they come in various sizes so you may purchase just the amount you need. Try to use a non-flammable stripper. It is useful to know the different types of chemical stripping agents. The strongest stripper is the Nitromors Original which is sold in yellow cans. This is pure liquid and not particularly suitable for vertical surfaces. Another Nitromors product is a gel stripper which is suitable for vertical surfaces because being a gel this tends to hang on to the wood rather than run down it to form a puddle at the bottom.

A fairly new idea is a stripping paste that you trowel on as if you were plastering a wall. This chemical is troweled on to the surface and left for a while. The whole application is then wiped off, taking the paint with it. The length of time you must leave the stripper on will depend on how much paint is on the wood. Use a trial area first to see how long the stripper needs to activate. The main advantage of this method is that you can apply the stripper and carry on with some other job, coming back to complete the stripping when the chemical has lifted the paint from the wood.

The chemicals already mentioned are available through most good hardware and DIY stores and there are, of course, many other makers of stripping agents. All will do the job of removing paint.

There is one chemical for stripping I have not mentioned so far and that is caustic soda. This is available from chemists, unlike the other types of stripping agents. Caustic soda should not be used on some types of wood as it will discolour the wood. Use caustic soda only on pine, elm and beech.

Precautions Good ventilation, as well as protection for the floor, is essential as some of these chemicals give off fumes. The best place to do this type of job is in the garden on a fine day where drips do not matter and there is, of course, plenty of ventilation. Caustic soda should only be used outside as you will find out later.

You will also need protection for your hands and eyes, as many of these chemicals will burn and can cause serious injury if splashed into the eyes. Use plastic gloves that will stretch high up your arms and an old jacket and apron to protect your clothes. Most important is a pair of clear safety spectacles or old glasses. These must be worn as soon as you start to pour out the chemical stripper.

One other useful tip when stripping is to have a bowl of water and an old towel handy to wash off any splashes on your face.

Also remove all handles and fittings before applying any stripper. These can be stripped separately.

Stripping paint First pour a small amount of a paint stripper like Nitromors into a paint kettle or an old tin. Replace the lid on the can. Do not screw the lid down tight as it is necessary for the chemical to 'breathe' to remain stable. Store the tin out of direct sunlight and out of reach of children.

Using an oldish 5 cm (2 in) paintbrush, apply a liberal coat of stripper onto the painted surface. If you watch the surface you will see bubbles begin to appear. The time this takes varies from article to article, but when the surface has bubbled all over, scrape the layer of paint off using a painter's broadknife. Drop the old paint into a metal bucket, not onto the floor as the softened paint will tread everywhere if it gets stuck to the bottom of your shoes.

Apply another coat of stripper to the surface and wait for it to activate. It is a good idea to be doing several pieces at once, working in rotation. For example, you can be scraping the paint from one drawer of a chest of drawers, while the others are activating. Generally one application of stripper will remove one layer of paint.

Keep on removing the coats of paint until you reach the bare wood. The last layer of paint may well need two applications of stripper, removing the last one with wire wool No 2 grade. Rub only with the grain, removing all tiny flecks of paint.

To strip handles and fittings, which have previously been removed, place each one in a vice or mole wrench, whilst you remove the paint or lacquer with a brass-haired wire brush. An excessive build-up of paint on mouldings can be difficult to remove, so extra stripper may be applied to them and left a little longer to activate. Then with a toothbrush, gently rub away the softened paint. Stubborn pieces can be eased away with a sharp chisel. Gently hold the chisel flat in the wood and push under the hardened paint. It is important for the handle to rest on the wood throughout this operation, otherwise there is a risk of the blade digging into the surface (Fig 2).

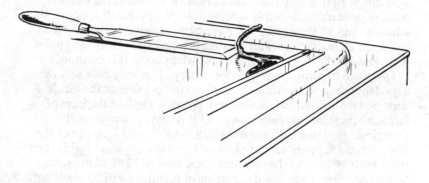

Fig 2 Easing away stubborn paint with a chisel

Another point to watch when stripping is to avoid the stripper making runs down other surfaces. The correct procedure is to start at the top and work down, taking extra care not to splash stripper onto the already finished surfaces. This would leave unsightly run lines, which are difficult to remove.

When the whole item has been stripped put it aside to allow it to dry thoroughly. Failure to do this will cause subsequent polish that is applied to dissolve.

Each type of chemical stripper has its own neutralising agent, usually methylated spirit or turpentine, and these will kill all traces of the chemical stripper.

Stripping with caustic soda   Caustic soda is a rather nasty chemical to use but it does have certain advantages over the ready-mixed strippers. But remember the previous advice on the types of wood it may be used for — that is, pine, elm and beech. It may only be used outside as its application requires quite a lot of water. Do not use it where you wish to grow plants, in fact over a gravel path or drive is a suitable place as caustic soda is also a good weedkiller.

Caustic soda usually comes in powder or flake form. Add one large handful to a litre (1¾ pints) of water for a fairly strong mix. Caustic soda will generate its own heat when added to water and will work much better when the solution is warm. The same safety precautions as previously mentioned are essential.

When working with mixed caustic soda, apply it with a sponge to the article being stripped. It is quite dramatic to see the way the caustic removes the old ..t, even from the most difficult mouldings. In this case the handles may be left on as the caustic mixture penetrates the most inaccessible places. Keep applying the solution until all traces of paint have been removed. Then with a hose-pipe or bucket of water remove all traces of caustic and paint. A good wash down is most important when using this method.

The piece of furniture is then left to dry. This may take several days depending on the time of year and the dryness of the air. It must be emphasised that before any polish is applied the item of furniture must be completely dry. As it is drying out you will sometimes find that salts from the caustic soda will seep out of the wood. If this happens let the piece of furniture dry thoroughly then apply malt vinegar to the affected area. This will kill all the salts. When the vinegar has dried the items of furniture will be ready for polishing.

To dispose of the caustic soda mixture, dig a hole in an area of the garden that is not used for planting. Fill in the hole to protect children and animals.

Commercial stripping   If you have a number of pine pieces of furniture to strip it may pay you to have them stripped commercially. In most towns there are companies specialising in stripping pine. The items to be stripped are immersed into a tank filled with a caustic soda mix. The piece of furniture is kept turning until the old paint has been removed. The article is then washed, sometimes using power washers, similar to those used by lorry chassis cleaning companies. This removes all traces of caustic soda.

Items such as doors, skirting boards and architraves are often taken to companies with large tanks that are able to cope with this type of stripping job.

Stripping clear finishes   The removal of clear finishes on wood is somewhat different from that of painted surfaces. Once again one has to evaluate the condition of the surface and whether you would be devaluing the item of furniture by the removal of its existing polish. If the surface is just dirty with only a few defects you could possibly refurbish the surface using the following recipe and technique. Mix together the following:

1 part linseed oil
1 part malt vinegar
1 part turpentine substitute
¼ part methylated spirit

Thoroughly mix these ingredients by putting them into a bottle and shaking well. Then using a coarse rag with the mixture applied to it, rub in a circular motion, removing the accumulation of dirt. Stubborn marks and dirt can be removed by using 000 wire wool instead of rag, taking great care not to cut right through the polished surface.

Usually a good wax finish after this treatment is all that is required to restore the item to its original condition. The important point here is that you must try to save the existing surface at all costs. Stripping off all the polish is only done as a last resort when, for instance, the surfaces are so far gone the only thing left is to remove all the old polish.

Time and care in removing all traces of dirt and polish will leave the wood a superb colour. This is especially true of old elm. The pleasure that comes from seeing the natural grains and colour of the wood coming through the dirt and restoring the item of furniture to the peak of condition gives you the greatest satisfaction.

Stripping a polished or varnished surface   Rubber or plastic gloves are essential because of the sticky nature of shellac polishes. Hands can be washed with methylated spirit but this tends to leave them dry, so use a good hand cream if you remove dirt from your hands with this method.

Removing polish should only be carried out in a well ventilated garage or workshop.

French polish can be removed using a variety of different solvents including the well known commercial chemical strippers already mentioned. Using methylated spirit and 0000 wire wool you can remove any french polish by gently rubbing with the grain of the wood. Another solvent that can be used is ammonia which is available from chemist shops and is a very good stripping agent, although the very strong pungent smell often prevents people from using it. Ammonia requires fan-drawn ventilation or needs to be used outside in the fresh air. Protection for the hands and eyes is essential. The main advantage of this chemical is that it leaves the wood a very good colour. It is very suitable for mahogany.

The mixture for general stripping is 190 ml ($\frac{1}{3}$ pint) of 880 concentrated ammonia to 4½ litres (1 gallon) of water. This mix may be diluted or strengthened according to the job in hand. One safety point here — when mixing any chemical with water, always pour the chemical into the water, never the other way round.

Varnishes and present-day finishes can be stripped by using a chemical stripper. Lay on a coat of stripper, wait until the surface bubbles then remove with a flat painter's broadknife. Finish with wire wool. If you find certain solvents do not activate then use one of the other types until you find the one that most easily removes the varnish. Wax polish that has become dirty by excessive build-up and spotted by water marks can be removed by saturating a ball of cloth in turpentine substitute and rubbing in a circular motion until the wax begins to dissolve. Keep turning the rag to make the removal of the wax easier. Failure to do this will cause the wax to build up on the rag and the surface will become smeared.

When using any kind of stripping agent there must be no excuse for untidiness, as some of these chemicals are flammable. Others give off unpleasant fumes or could cause skin irritation should they come in contact with either the hands or face. So, as you finish using any piece of rag, wire wool, etc, throw it into a metal container and dispose of it in the dustbin at the first opportunity.

Quick tips

1   Clean moulding and carved work by using vinegar and rubbing with an old toothbrush.

2   A good washing-up liquid, diluted 50/50 with warm water, will remove stubborn dirt and grime using an old toothbrush.

3   A square of old glass will make an ideal scraper for use on old polished surfaces. Use a piece approximately 13 cm × 8 cm (5 in ×.3 in). Stick adhesive tape around the edges not being used to protect the hands.

4   Wire wool clogs very easily when removing old paint and varnish. So scrape off as much as possible with a scraper and clear the wire wool by banging it on a hard surface. This will remove much of the old paint or varnish.

Veneers

Veneers are thin sheets of wood used for covering over a carcass of thick wood. The idea is that veneers of the more expensive and decorative woods can be used to simulate solid wood at a lower cost. In addition, the method by which it is cut (Fig 1) produces a more decorative grain. There are hundreds of different wood veneers to choose from but you will have to buy the more exotic types from companies specialising in veneers. I find the ones available from local DIY stores are not generally suitable for repairs to old furniture and the selection is not very good.

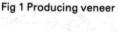

Fig 1 Producing veneer

Removing veneer

A good source of veneer is furniture broken beyond repair and veneer obtained in this way can be used to restore a more desirable item.

The method of removing old veneer is quite simple. First set the temperature of an ordinary electric flat iron between medium and high; lay the board from which you wish to remove the veneer on a flat surface and cover with a sheet of brown paper. When the iron has reached the correct temperature put it on the paper and iron it, keeping the iron moving to avoid scorching. Covering an area of approximately 900 sq cm (1 sq ft) at a time, you will find that the heat of the iron will melt the glue that is holding the veneer. Soon the glue will be soft enough for you to be able to insert a long knife or a painter's broadknife (Fig 2) between the veneer and the carcass. Take great care not to split the veneer. By gently sliding the knife between the veneer and the carcass you will soon be able to lift small areas and as each section is lifted you can move on to the next. You need only just melt the glue enough to be able to lift the veneer and with care you should be able to remove quite large pieces that are quite suitable for re-use.

Fig 2 Lifting old veneer

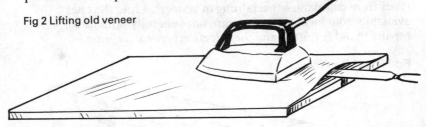

Fig 3 Sandwiching veneer to prevent curling

¾ in (18 mm) chipboard or similar

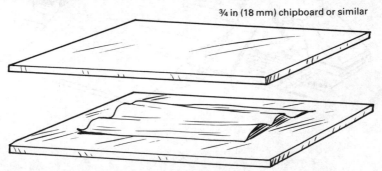

After the veneer has been removed sandwich it between two pieces of flat timber to stop it curling (Fig 3). Any glue that remains on the under side of the veneer must be scraped off with a steel cabinet-maker's scraper before the veneer is applied to another carcass. If you have judged the heat right you will hardly have disturbed the existing polish so when you use this veneer for repairing another item you could save yourself a lot of work matching up the polish to the existing wood and it will only require the minimum amount of touching up. I will always use old veneers whenever possible because new veneer requires considerable touching up and polishing to make a good match to the existing wood.

Removing blisters from veneer

It is quite common on old furniture to find a blister in the veneer. The cause of this could be one of several things. It is possible that damp has caused the veneer to lift. Alternatively, when the veneer was originally laid the glue may have dried too quickly or a spot may have been missed altogether. There are several methods you can try for removing blisters.

The first is to use the iron again, at a medium temperature, working as before with a piece of brown paper covering the affected area. Press down hard whilst moving the iron backwards and forwards. It is critical not to iron for too long in any one place as all you want to do is to reactivate the bonding glue. If you do iron for too long you will crystallise and destroy the bonding glue, and if this happens you will make a small job into a major one.

When you feel the glue has softened remove the iron and, working quickly, press down on the blister with the edge of a piece of smooth wood and rub the blister flat (Fig 4). Leaving the brown paper in place, weight down the blister with books or some other heavy object and leave for 8-12 hours. It is advisable then to leave the item for a week or so as sometimes the blister will reappear after the wood has settled down to room temperature.

Should the blister reappear, you should proceed as follows. Using a sharp modeller's knife slit the blister along the middle, cutting with the grain. Try and dust out any dirt or grit with a fine brush or vacuum cleaner. Using a thin knife-blade dipped in a PVA glue, cover the whole area underneath the veneer with a film of glue. Then, using the edge of a hammer or a smooth piece of

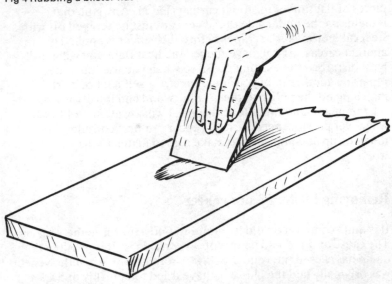

Fig 4 Rubbing a blister flat

wood, squeeze out any excess glue and wipe off from the surface.
Using a piece of greaseproof paper, cover the blister and apply
weights to hold it down for 8–12 hours. This method will usually
cure all blisters and the cut you made in the veneer will be
completely hidden when the glue has dried. Then all that remains
is to apply a gentle wax polish over the area.

Loose veneer

Often veneer becomes loose, usually at the edges. This type of job
is quite simple. The essential thing to do is to clean any dirt and
grime from the area to be glued. This is done by gently lifting the
veneer with a thin knife and scraping out any debris before
applying the glue. Always protect any surface you are going to
cramp by first covering with greaseproof paper. This protects the
finished wood surface by preventing the glue from sticking to it.
On top of the greaseproof paper use scrap pieces of wood so as not
to bruise the polished surface when the cramps are applied (Fig 5).

Fig 5 Cramping veneer while the glue dries

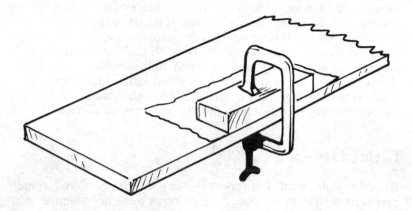

Replacing a section of veneer

If a section of veneer is missing or there is a defect, like a cigarette burn, that you cannot disguise then the veneer will have to be replaced. Taking, for example, a burn in the wood you will have to cut out this piece of veneer. To do the job you will need a thin, sharp modeller's knife or scalpel and a steel straight-edge. Cut a diamond pattern in the veneer, the defect being in the centre (Fig 6). This type of cut is less noticeable than one with square edges. It is most important that the cut goes right through the veneer. Failure to do this will result in breaking the surrounding edges when you come to lift out the defective veneer.

When the cuts have been made correctly, lift out the diamond shape with a small sharp chisel, starting from the middle so as not to bruise or disturb the surrounding veneer. Gently prise away the veneer, making sure that you remove all small pieces from the corners of the diamond shape. Remove any traces of old glue from the surface of the carcass, using a sharp-pointed knife.

The next part of the operation is to take some care to find a suitable piece of veneer to match. Having done so, place a piece of tracing paper over the diamond cut-out and hold it in position with masking tape whilst you rub over the surface of the diamond with a soft pencil to give you a tracing of the piece that has been cut out (Fig 7). This is then removed and transferred to the piece of veneer you are going to fit in. You may find it easier to paste the tracing onto the veneer before cutting. If so, when the paste is sufficiently set, cut through the tracing paper and veneer (Fig 8), using the same sharp knife and steel rule. If you have been very accurate the diamond-shaped piece should fit with hardly a line showing. This piece of veneer is then glued and cramped into position in the way already described. When the glue has set the surfaces are sanded down until the two areas are smooth and flat.

Laying a veneer

Before applying a sheet of veneer to a carcass surface there is some preparatory work to be done. As previously mentioned, veneer is cut from a log in thin sheets so when you purchase your veneer you may find that it is not flat. Many people who have ordered it through the mail are quite concerned on discovering this but there really is nothing to worry about. Before you are ready to lay your veneer you must first dampen both sides of it with a wet sponge and then lay it between two pieces of board. Chipboard is ideal for this as it will act rather like blotting paper, absorbing the moisture from the veneer. Several sheets of veneer may be laid down at a time; these should be left for three to four hours. Weights may be applied to the top of the boards, if required, to hold the veneer flat. After a few hours it may be removed and you will find that it is now flat and very much more pliable.

Veneers, such as burr walnut, will look like a rough mountain range before this process and may need a little longer between the boards, but when they are taken out they will be as flat as a pancake. You may also find holes and splits in some of the more wild-grained veneers. These have to be filled in with other matching veneers after they have been laid.

Gluing   Whilst the veneer is being flattened you can carry on with some of the other preparatory work, like scoring the surface of the carcass to provide a key for the glue. Different people have different ideas on which is the best glue for sticking down veneers. My favourite is the well established animal glue, or Scotch glue.

Before applying any glue to either the carcass or veneer it is

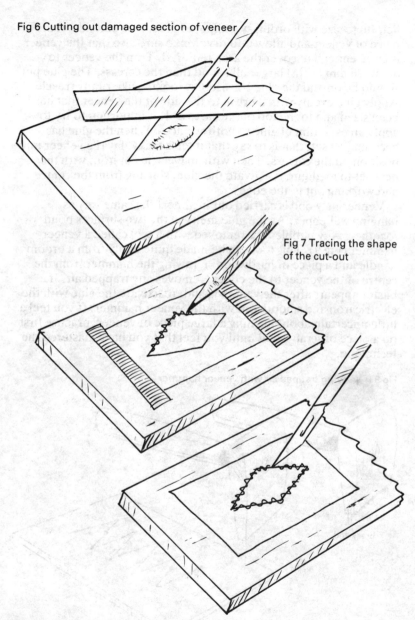

Fig 6 Cutting out damaged section of veneer

Fig 7 Tracing the shape of the cut-out

Fig 8 Cutting the required shape from veneer

helpful to size with ordinary wallpaper glue. Size one side of the piece of veneer and allow it to dry. Make sure also that the veneer is large enough to cover the area required. Trim the veneer to about 18 mm (¾ in) larger all round than the carcass. The glue pot should be on and the glue consistency looking like runny treacle. Apply glue evenly with a brush to the side of the veneer that has been sized and to the top of the carcass. It is important to try to apply an even film of glue to both surfaces. When the glue has become just set, that is to say that it feels tacky, lay the veneer into position on the carcass. Then with an electric flat iron, with the heat set to medium, reactivate the glue, starting from the centre and working out to the edges.

Veneering wood is carried out in almost the same way as hanging wallpaper. As the glue melts so the two surfaces bond together. Any bubbles are removed with a tool called a veneer hammer (Fig 9). This tool can be made quite easily from a broom handle and a piece of hardwood. Drawing the hammer from the centre of the veneer to the edges, removes any trapped air. If a blister appears after the veneer is laid, reactivate the glue with the electric iron and smooth out with the veneer hammer. If you feel a little uncertain about tackling a large piece of veneer, practise first on a piece of scrap wood until you feel that you have mastered the technique.

Fig 9 Removing trapped air with veneer hammer

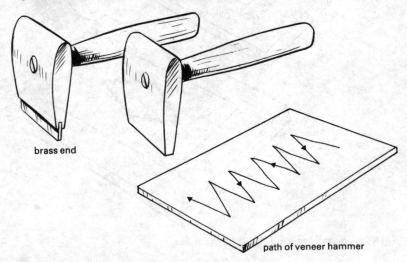

brass end

path of veneer hammer

Joining two pieces of veneer When this has to be done, lay the first piece, then position the second piece so that it overlaps by 18 mm (¾ in) the first section and stick it down. When the second piece is firmly bonded cut through the overlap using a steel straight-edge and a sharp knife or scalpel (Fig 10). Remove the

Fig 10 Removing veneer overlap

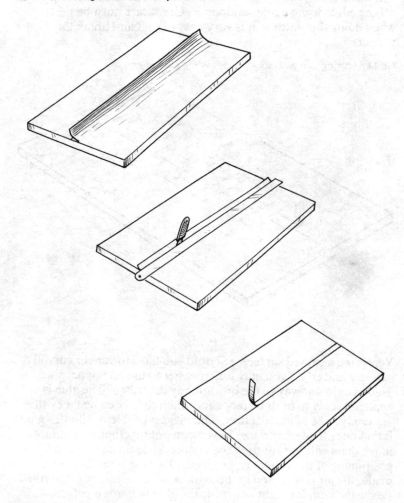

two strips of veneer that have now been cut off and rub down the two areas beside the cut with the veneer hammer to form what should be a perfect join. Using brown sticky paper over the join (Fig 11), hold down the two edges until the glue has dried. This paper is easy to remove by damping it with a sponge when the veneer has dried completely. The outside edges can now be trimmed. This is done with a sharp knife and block plane, finishing off the edges using a fine sandpaper. Great care must be taken when doing this because it is very easy to split and break the veneer.

Fig 11 Securing join with sticky paper while glue dries

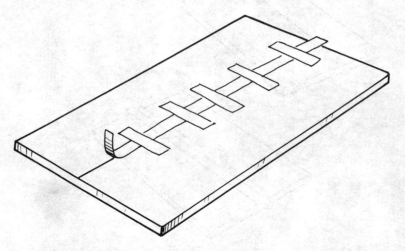

Veneering a curved surface   Should you have to veneer curved surfaces and edges you may find it easier to use an impact glue, used in a similar way to the one already described. The glue is applied evenly to both surfaces and when they become tacky they are ready to be stuck together. The biggest problem with this glue is that once the two surfaces have been put together you cannot move them without splitting the veneer, so great care in the positioning of the veneer is required. Once the bond has been made, the air is removed in the same manner as already described. Leave the item for eight hours for the glue to harden before attempting to trim off excess veneer.

Glue film   Recent advances in glue research have brought about the development of what is effectively a veneer of glue. This is a film of glue that is layed onto a roll of greaseproof paper and you buy this by the length from a roll. It is very economical as you simply cut off the amount you require.

You lay veneer using glue film in the following manner. Cut the film 12 mm (½ in) larger than the area required and lay it glue side down onto the carcass surface. Then with an iron set at about medium temperature, iron the film from the centre outwards. Through the paper you will see the glue melting and bonding on to the carcass. When the glue has melted and stuck to the whole of the carcass remove the protective paper. Make absolutely sure the glue has bonded to the whole of the surface. Place the veneer on top of the glue film and cover with the paper removed from the film. You now iron down the veneer, melting the film and bonding the veneer to the carcass. Work in exactly the same way as already described from the centre outwards until the whole area has been bonded. You may use the veneer hammer for final pressure in laying the veneer.

All these methods will bond veneer to any carcass work. Choose the one you can manage best. If you are not sure if you can attempt a large piece, practise veneering scrapwood until you find the technique that suits you best. It is very disheartening to spoil a large piece of expensive veneer so time spent in practice is not wasted.

Staining and Polishing

Often people who are capable of restoring and repairing woodwork on an old piece of furniture dread the final operation of staining and polishing the repaired piece. There are, of course, several stages and many techniques involved in achieving a finish that should have the look and feel of satin. If you think all there is to polishing is dipping a brush into a pot of varnish then you will be very disappointed. Brushing on varnish is fine for a pine ceiling or window frame but not for producing a superb finish on an old piece of furniture.

French polishing is a job that requires infinite patience and time because each coat of polish has to dry before you can apply the next one. This means, of course, that the job you are doing may take up to a week to finish. Nevertheless, with patience the result will be well worth all the time and effort you have put into it. French polishing is one of those jobs where you need to practise on a small off-cut whilst you learn the techniques of applying the polish. The reward for taking this trouble will be a superb-looking piece of furniture. Mistakes on scrap wood can be rectified but imagine your reaction when you are perhaps up to the final part of polishing a piece of furniture and you make a mistake — which, I admit, has happened to me — and you realise that the only solution is to remove all the polish and start again. A professional french polisher has to serve an apprenticeship of five years, so do not expect to be an expert within a few hours. Practice is the word and by taking your time you will finally be able to achieve a finish on furniture that will be admired by all your friends. Many local evening centres hold night classes on french polishing so why not enrol and learn from a master craftsman?

Before you start to apply any polish there are certain jobs that have to be done to ensure a good finish to your work. The wood the polish is to be applied to must be sanded down so there are no bumps and defects in the wood. If new pieces of wood have been let in then these will have to be smoothed down level with the surrounding wood. If the sun has bleached the wood you may wish to darken it with a stain.

Removing dirt   Often a piece of furniture is dirty; if this is the case there is no need to strip it. Using the reviver recipe described in the chapter on stripping furniture, gently rub the surfaces with a rag to remove the dirt. If the dirt is ingrained in the wood you may use a fine wire wool, grade No 0000. Keep the wire wool well lubricated with the reviver and rub in the direction of the grain, lifting out all the old dirt. Do make sure not to cut right through the old polish as this will leave the surface looking patchy. What actually happens when using reviver is that the mixture removes the dirt and the methylated spirit just dissolves the top layer of polish. So when the surface has been cleaned all over and wiped down with a rag dampened with turpentine it will only need a good wax polishing to bring the piece of furniture up to the way it looked when it was made.

The only recommendation I would make is to use a rag rather than wire wool whenever possible. But when using either of these keep turning over the rag or wire wool so that it does not clog and cut right through the polish. It is one of the most rewarding jobs to do because you see the colour and grain of the wood come up through the years of dirt. Surface dirt caused by a build-up of wax and grime can be removed with a rag soaked in turpentine and then squeezed out leaving just enough moisture for you to lift off the old wax and dirt. Dispose of all the old rags in a dustbin outside the house because most of the mixtures like turpentine, methylated spirit, linseed oil and commercial polishes are flammable so it makes good sense not to leave the rags lying about on a workshop or shed floor.

Methylated spirit in its concentrated form can also be used for the removal of dirt but exercise great care when using it because it will dissolve french polish very quickly. Neutralise methylated spirit, as soon as the dirt has been removed, with turpentine soaked into a rag. Failure to neutralise any stripping chemical can cause the new polish to bubble, so after neutralising leave the piece of furniture to dry thoroughly. Leave for eight hours before applying any stains or polish.

Removing old polish

If the old polish has deteriorated to the point where it cannot be
revived, the only alternative is to strip off all the old surfaces using
one of the chemical strippers mentioned in the chapter on
stripping furniture. Most old polishes can be removed using
ammonia. Pour $\frac{1}{3}$ strong ammonia to $\frac{2}{3}$ water, and *always* add the
ammonia to the water. Wear old clothes and protection for the
hands and eyes, that is, rubber gloves and safety glasses. Because
of the very pungent smell with ammonia I strongly advise you to
do this job outside or in a well ventilated area and well away from
children and animals. Apply the ammonia to the wood with a 25
mm (1 in) paintbrush, then with a ball of fine wire wool No. 0000
and rubbing in a circular motion, gently strip away the old polish.
Try the operation first on a small section that is not easily seen.
Never start on the middle of a table but try first at the bottom of a
leg to ensure you are using the correct stripper. If you find the
solution is not removing the polish add a drop more ammonia until
the polish begins to strip off easily.

When all the old polish has been removed, neutralise the wood
using cold water. Stripping with ammonia gives a good colour to
most woods and is most suitable for mahogany. Always remember
to store the bottles of ammonia far out of the reach of children in a
cool place with a distinctive label to indicate the contents. This
advice applies to all chemicals that you are liable to use and
whatever chemical stripper or reviver you use.

Removing grease marks

These can be removed using a domestic electric iron and talcum
powder. Sprinkle a generous amount of powder on the affected
area and cover with several layers of tissue paper. Warm the
tissues and talc with the iron on a low setting. The temperature of
the iron will draw out the grease soaking into both the talcum
powder and tissues. Great care must be taken if working on a
veneered surface as the heat of the iron may lift the veneer.

Removing dents

Whilst you have the iron handy you can remove any dents in the wood. Place a thick damp cloth over the dent and with the iron set at cool, and using only the tip, place it exactly on the dent (Fig 1). The moisture and heat will cause the wood to swell, thus removing the dent.

Fig 1 Removing dents

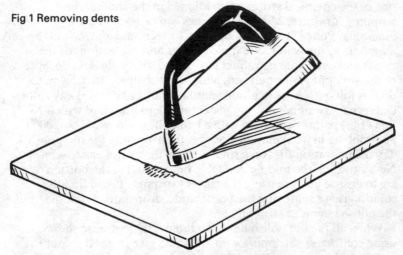

Removing stains

You will, of course, have to remove any stains perhaps caused by ink or water. These should be removed with great care before the final sanding. Ink is one of the most common stains on wood especially on old desks or writing tables. It can usually be removed by one of the following methods. Practise first on a scrap of wood that has become stained. To start with, try a combination of vinegar and Milton, which is a liquid sold by chemists for sterilising babies' feeding bottles, etc. Dab a cotton bud dipped in vinegar on to the ink stain, then immediately follow this with a dab of Milton. Repeat this process until the stain disappears. Wash off any residue with cold water. The piece must, of course, be left to dry before any polish is applied.

Oxalic acid, available from chemists in crystal form, may be saturated in warm water and used in the same way as already described. Some of the crystals may not dissolve: this is a sign that the mixture has reached its maximum strength and is ready for use. Remember the rules about handling chemicals — wear glasses and gloves for protection at all times.

Should none of these methods work you can try diluted nitric acid. Your chemist will mix this for you. It should be around a 5% mix. If you mix this yourself, remember the golden rule: add acid to water.

There are many other patent recipes for removing ink stains. I have tried the methods described and usually one of them will remove all traces of an ink stain. In fact, one will usually remove most types of stain so do experiment, taking great care to apply the chemical only to the affected area and wash away any surplus with clean water.

Sanding

If the wood is not perfectly smooth, sand it down with fine sandpaper and a block (Fig 2). A sanding block can be easily made using a scrap piece of wood 75 mm (3 in) wide, 125 mm (5 in) long and 25 mm (1 in) thick. Stick to the underside a piece of cork or lino and smooth off all the sharp edges. Cork will make a softer bed for the sandpaper to lie on so there will be less chance of grit scratching the surface of the wood.

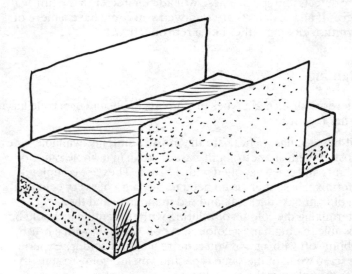

Fig 2 Sanding block

Always use the sanding block in the direction of the grain. Do not use a coarse grit sandpaper. Start off with a No F2 Medium and finish with a No 1 Extra Fine. There is often lots of confusion when using sandpaper. Many professional tradesmen call it 'glasspaper' and perhaps this is the correct term to use. Glasspaper, as its name implies, is made from crushed glass bonded onto a sheet of paper. Another abrasive paper is called 'garnet paper'; again, the name comes from the stone from which the grit is made. This type is more expensive than glasspaper but it is very much more durable and less liable to clog. It is a most suitable paper for finishing by hand so I would recommend you use this. Silicon carbide papers, sometimes known as 'wet and dry', are very useful for extra fine surfaces and they can be used damp — not wet. Dampened with water, acting as a lubricant, very fine finishes can be achieved. They are long-wearing and can be used on all types of metal. All other glass and garnet papers must be stored in a dry place. If you try to use them damp you will pull off all the grit and score the surface of the piece of furniture.

Wire wool can also be used for finishing wood to a fine and smooth surface. Use only the very fine grade No 0000. When sanding smooth a piece of old furniture never try to remove all the tiny defects and spots. These will add character to the finished piece. If all the defects are removed you could have a piece of furniture looking rather like a reproduction.

Staining

There are three main types of stain available and everyone has his or her favourite.

Oil-based stains   These are the most commonly available type. Most of them are petroleum-based, come in a whole range of colours and can be applied with a brush. They are completely intermixable so there is no need to buy a tin of every colour. Buy a tin of light oak, dark oak and red mahogany and then by intermixing the colours or diluting with turpentine it should be possible to obtain most colours. Apply the stain with a brush, rubbing off with a rag if you require a lighter colour. Experiment on scrap wood of the same type that you are going to stain to make sure the colour is the one you want.

One disadvantage with this type of stain is that the oil will lay on the surface of the wood and not give very good adhesion to polish. In addition, oil-based stains tend to fade if the piece of furniture is kept in bright sunlight. Once the stain has been applied it must be left to stand for 24 hours for it to dry thoroughly. Staining and polishing is always best done in a warm room. Any dampness in the air will delay the drying times and possibly bloom the polish after it has been applied.

Spirit stains   These are not so readily available, but they can be purchased from specialist suppliers. (See 'List of suppliers'.) Spirit stains are made from refined methylated spirit mixed with dye and a small amount of shellac. They can also be purchased in a large range of colours and can be intermixed to produce the required colour. These stains are applied with a brush and you will find that you will have to work quite fast because this type will penetrate wood very quickly. It is also easy to produce smears and streaks if you do not work quickly. Spirit stain has one other disadvantage and that is it will tend to be absorbed more quickly into the soft parts of the wood, often giving a blotchy look.

You can make your own spirit stain by adding a powdered stain of the chosen colour to methylated spirit. The depth of colour will depend on the amount of dye you add to the methylated spirit. Add to this mixture a small quantity of french polish; this will seal the polish when it has been applied to the wood. If the french polish is not added you will find when you start to apply the finishing coat of polish later on you may lift some of the stain out. This is caused by the french polish having the same spirit base as the stain. The one big advantage of spirit stain is that it dries very quickly, so you can start polishing sooner.

Water stains   You can very easily make up this type yourself. It has the great advantage of being both the cheapest type and the most economical as you only need to mix up as much as you require for each job. There are dozens of different coloured dyes so any combination of colours can be made including green, pink, purple and so on. You can buy these powered dyes from specialist companies in small quantities to suit your own pocket. You should start off by having the following colours: red mahogany, brown mahogany, black, walnut, dark oak and light oak. With these colours you will be able to match almost any type of wood and restore the piece of furniture to its original colour.

To mix water stain you must first heat up some water. Meanwhile, pour the powdered dye into a plastic bucket. When the water is hot pour it over the powder and stir thoroughly, making absolutely sure the powder has dissolved. You may add just a drop of Ammonia 880 to the mix. This will give the stain a better penetration when applied to the wood. When the mixture has been thoroughly stirred, put it to one side to cool. If water stain is used hot the result may look blotchy as the hot water causes uneven penetration, soaking deeper into the softer areas of the wood.

Before applying any water stain to a prepared article you must first dampen the surface of the wood with a wet sponge to raise the grain. Apply a wet sponge to all surfaces of the wood; the grain will rise as it dries. When the wood has completely dried, the surface is sanded smooth again using a fine-grade glasspaper. If you apply a water stain on a finished piece of wood without first wetting it with plain water, the grain will rise in exactly the same way leaving a rough surface. When you then come to glasspaper the surface you will find that it looks spotty due to the raised areas being rubbed down more than the lower-lying sections. So, to summarise, always wet the sanded surface first with clear water, put the item aside to dry and then finally sand the surface flat and smooth before applying the water stain. It is only when using water stains that this procedure is required.

After the wood has been treated in this way and sanded smooth, the water stain can be applied. Use an old rag dipped in the stain and rub well into the wood, starting by going across the grain and finishing with long even strokes with the grain. Excess stain may be wiped off with a clean rag. Set aside to dry and leave for eight hours. If after this period of time the colour is the right shade, leave the item for a further eight hours to dry thoroughly. If after the first eight hours, however, you wish to darken the wood you simply apply another coat of stain and leave for a further eight hours to dry.

Water stains can be lightened slightly when they have been applied to the wood. Using a clean damp rag, wipe evenly over the surface of the wood to reactivate and remove the surplus stain. Once the desired colour is achieved leave the item for eight to fourteen hours in a warm room for it to dry. The wood will then be ready for the final operation of grain filling and polishing.

Grain filling

Wood, like our skin, has pores and to obtain a perfect finish on wood you will have to fill them in. The old method of doing this was to use plaster of Paris and rose-pink powdered dye mixed with water to a paste. This was applied to the wood and then sanded smooth. Often when an old piece of furniture has been stripped you will find a white fleck in the wood. This is a remnant of the old grain filler. It will look white because the dye, over the years, will have faded.

Nowadays commercial grain fillers are available. Choose one the same colour as the wood you have stained. Alternatively you may add powdered stain to achieve the correct colour in which case thorough mixing will be required as any part of the filler that has not been mixed properly will show up in the grain. When the grain filler is mixed to the required colour, apply it to the surface of the wood using a piece of hessian or coarse rag, rubbing hard across the grain so as to fill all the pores in the wood. Rubbing along the grain tends to pull out the filler. Try to leave as little filler as possible on the surface because when the filler has dried it has to be sanded down smooth with a fine glasspaper, rubbing along the grain. When the whole of the wood has been filled and sanded we can then start the last and perhaps the most important part of the job — polishing.

Polishing

Everyone at some time has heard of the term 'french polish'. Very few people realise the intricacies involved in producing that superb finish on old pieces of furniture and let us not pretend that french polishing is easy. It is hard, time-consuming work right from the beginning, by that I mean the collection of the raw material.

French polish is obtained from shellac. By far the largest supplier is India where a small insect called a 'lac' (Latin *Cocus lacca*) lives. It feeds on a substance, similar to resin, that is exuded from the stems of a small bush. During the course of the lac's life it sheds its shell, hence the name 'shellac'. This substance is collected and placed in porous bags and hung in the sun. As the substance melts it drips onto the ground and forms what are known as 'buttons' and these are then collected and exported throughout the world. Since it was a Frenchman who discovered that shellac could be dissolved in methylated spirit, the name 'french polish' arose. By bleaching shellac with oxalic acid you can produce a white polish and by adding powdered dyes you can obtain virtually any colour. So, in all, french polish is one of the most versatile and useful polishes available. I ought to make one point clear, however, namely that french polish is a fairly recent development. It was not introduced until the 19th century, so it should not be used on furniture from earlier periods.

Preparation   Before applying any french polish to the surface of the wood you will need to decide the colour of the polish. The most common ones used are pale french polish and dark french polish. Once you have made your decision, pour some of the polish into a small clean and dry sauce bottle or something similar. Pierce a hole about 3 mm (⅛ in) in the top and screw it back on the bottle. The next thing you need is called a 'rubber' (Fig 3). This is used for applying the polish to the wood and it is made in the following manner.

Take a piece of cotton sheet about the size of a gentleman's handkerchief and onto this lay some cotton wadding or cotton wool approximately 150 mm (6 in) square. Fold the two corners of the wadding to form a pear shape. Fold the cotton sheet over the wadding and twist the sheet tightly at the wider end (Fig 4). Pull the rubber into shape by forming it in the hands. The rubber should fit snugly into the palm of your hand with the pointed end towards your fingers. The rubber must always retain this shape, the pointed end being very important because it is used for polishing into corners and mouldings.

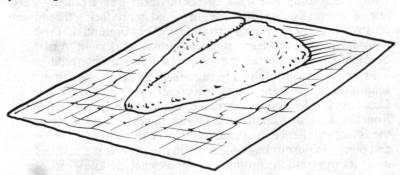

Fig 3 Making the rubber for french polishing

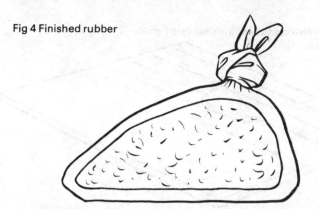

Fig 4 Finished rubber

When you feel the rubber is to your satisfaction you can then untwist the end and charge the wadding with polish from the bottle. You never apply the polish to the bottom of the rubber. At the first charging you will find that the wadding will soak up most of the polish but fold the wadding back into the outer cloth and twist the end until the polish oozes out of the cloth. If the polish fails to appear then the wadding will have to be recharged. Do not overload the wadding with too much polish at a time. With the pointed part of the rubber to the front of your hand gently twist the end. You should find this will bring the polish through to the surface of the rubber. When you are quite satisified that you have acquired this technique you are ready to start applying the polish to the wood, of course making quite sure that the wood is completely free from dust.

First stage   The rubber is used following the direction of the grain in long even strokes starting at one end and working your way along to the other (Fig 5). Always remove the rubber from the wood at the end of each stroke. It is most difficult to explain the correct amount of pressure required when applying the polish, and finding this out can only be done by practice. Remember that by pressing down too hard on the rubber will cause the polish to flood out so that on the return stroke you tend to pull it off again. Keep going along the grain until the whole surface has been covered with polish. You will find that by the time you have finished covering the surface and recharged the rubber, if necessary, the first coat has almost dried. I should also mention that french polishing needs to be done in a warm, well ventilated room as a damp atmosphere will cause the polish to bloom.

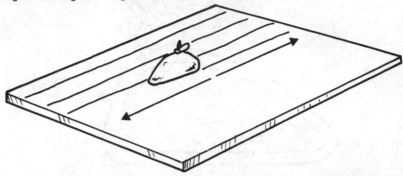

Fig 5 Polishing with long strokes in direction of grain

Just before applying the second coat of polish to the wood dab a small amount of linseed oil to the bottom of the rubber. Do not use boiled linseed. The oil is used as a lubricant to help the rubber glide over the surface of the wood. It also helps prevent the rubber from dragging but use the oil with extreme care because it has to be removed from the surface a little later, and if too much oil is used it will in time cause the surface polish to sweat, leaving it looking dull and rough. So all you need is a dab of linseed oil on the bottom of the rubber. This can be applied with the end of your finger.

After having applied two or three coats of polish with strokes going the whole length of the wood, you should then start using shorter strokes, say 300 – 375 mm (12–15 in) in length working across the width of the wood (Fig 6). After reaching the two edges

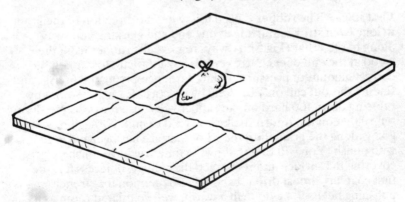

Fig 6 Polishing across width of wood

start another section just touching the first and so on until the whole area has been covered. Do not forget the dab of linseed oil to keep the rubber bottom lubricated. As the polish in the rubber is used up more pressure is required to squeeze it out. Do not press down too hard or you will remove the polish already applied.

The next coat of polish is applied in the manner that most people think of as loops and figures of eight. With the rubber loaded with polish, start at one end of the wood and work across the surface in a circular motion. On reaching the opposite side of the wood move down so that the next loops just touch the ones already applied. Proceed down the whole length of the wood (Fig 7). On reaching the end start again over the already applied loops. This time use a figure of eight pattern. Keep applying the polish in this way until all the polish in the rubber has been used. The reason for all these loops and figures of eight is to keep the polish as level as possible. If you kept applying the polish in straight lines you would finish up with a ridged and uneven surface. By using the above method you will find the surface of the polish fairly even.

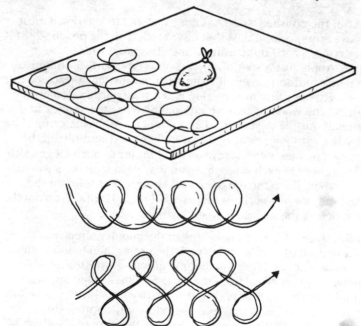

Fig 7 Polishing in loops and figures of eight

By this time you will have had to charge the rubber with polish about three times. Each time you fill the rubber with polish it is known as 'one rubber', so up to now three rubbers will have been used and the grain will have been completely filled and will look level. Fill the rubber with polish but do not apply any linseed oil, for this time you must remove any excess oil from the surface of the wood. This is done by using long strokes up and down the wood. Start off by pressing lightly and gradually build up the pressure until the polish in the rubber has been used. The work must then be set aside to dry for a couple of days. Do not be impatient to try to build up all the polish in one go as this is sure to bring disappointment.

Up to this point what you have done is to apply several layers of polish to the surface of the wood. This laying down a good base of polish is called 'bodying in' or 'bodying up'. If you now go on through the following stages you can, if you wish, finish up with what is known as a piano finish. But most furniture does not require this high degree of polish and it would look wrong in most cases.

After the polished wood has been allowed to stand you must remove any specks of dust that have settled on the polish whilst it was drying. This is done using a fine glasspaper such as flour paper. Apply just a spot of linseed oil on the surface to lubricate the paper and to prevent it from cutting into the surface of the polish. Remove any nibs or ridges but take care in doing so. Dust off the wood to remove any debris from the surface and you are ready for the next stage. I should mention that after finishing polishing with your rubber it can be kept soft and pliable by putting it in a jar with a screw-on lid. I prefer to put a clean cloth on my rubber at each stage, but you may wish to make a whole new rubber. Keep the old ones as they are very useful for the initial stages when perhaps you are picking up more dirt from the wood before the surface is coated with polish.

Second stage Carry on polishing in the manner already described. Start with working with the grain, then to loops and figures of eight and finish with long up-and-down strokes to remove any linseed oil from the surface. This second application should take three rubbers. Set aside to dry for a further 24 hours. If you require a piano finish you should apply another three rubbers in exactly the same way, leaving the item to stand for 24 hours between each application.

Final stage   If you have been following these instructions and do the same with the next part of the procedure you will see that all your labours will be more than worthwhile. The hardened surface of the polish has its final light rub-over with flour paper, not forgetting to lubricate the bottom with a dab of linseed oil. When the wood has been dusted off and is perfectly clean, use one more rubber of polish, applied in loops and figures of eight, finishing off by removing all the linseed oil in the direction of the grain.

Charge up the rubber again, this time using a mixture of one half french polish and one half methylated spirit. Mix these accurately before applying to the rubber. Work out two or three rubbers over the surface using loops and figures of eight. By the time you are on your last rubber you will notice that the surface of the polish is beginning to clear and all the slightly uneven marks are beginning to disappear. Put this rubber into your sealed jar for later use.

You now have to make a completely new rubber in exactly the same way as before, only this time fold the cotton fabric over twice. The cotton wadding in the centre of the rubber is soaked with methylated spirit and then almost all the spirit is squeezed out; this is most important. The rubber should never be wet, for this will dissolve the applied polish causing it to sag and spoil several hours of hard work. Rub the clean spirit-filled rubber up and down your bare arm until it feels just damp. Using no linseed oil, the rubber is then applied to the work and used in exactly the same way as applying the polish. You will now notice that the surface of the work is becoming bright and clean. As the rubber begins to dry out, fold over the clean cotton and finish off with long strokes in the direction of the grain to what should be a superb finish.

I must just stress once more that french polishing is easy to write about but nothing will give you the feel of it except practice and experience, so do not give up if things go wrong. Start off on scrap pieces of wood and progress to small items of furniture before undertaking any large project. This way I feel sure you will be able to produce the beautiful finishes that one sees on some lovely old furniture.

Upholstering a Simple Seat

Evening classes throughout the length and breadth of Britain are inundated by people wishing to learn how to upholster. If you think seriously about it, it is no good making a super job of repairing and repolishing a chair and then spoiling the whole effect by poor upholstery.

One of the easiest upholstery jobs to do is the drop-in seat that has no springs for you to fight with. After you have removed the seat from the chair, search for a number. Each chair will be numbered and this will correspond with a number on the drop-in seat. The number is usually a roman numeral cut into the back of the chair and hidden from view when the seat is in position. If by chance there is no number then mark each chair and seat as you remove them.

Before you start removing the old covers and webbing lay out a piece of polythene or an old sheet as this job can be rather dusty. The old stuffing and fabrics are then easily contained when following this procedure. If you have never done upholstery before you will find it a great help to have a writing pad to make any notes as you remove each layer of a covering.

Removing the old materials Start stripping off the old materials from the bottom. You should find the webbing covered by a piece of hessian. This will be tacked down and, of course, these tacks will all have to be removed. Make a jig (Fig 1) for holding the seat whilst you remove these tacks. Alternatively have someone hold the seat whilst you remove the tacks, making sure that the person's hands are clear of the tools you are using. The tacks can be removed with an old screwdriver, and I mean an old one, or you can purchase a tack lifter. There are several different types available (Fig 2). Place the edge of the tool against the head of the tack and with a sharp tap from a wood mallet lift it out. When these tacks come out they seem to be attracted to turn-ups, carpets, pockets and the bottom of your shoes so try and keep these from flying everywhere. An old box or tin is ideal for putting them in until all the stripping is done.

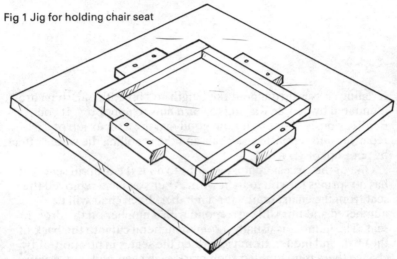

Fig 1 Jig for holding chair seat

After having removed the hessian you will be able to see the old webbing and interior of the chair. The next operation is to remove the outer fabrics; there may be several layers of these. The tacks will have to be removed in the same manner with the tack lifter. Do this holding the frame in a vice or with the help of a willing assistant holding the frame steady.

Place the layers of fabric in a pile in the order you take them off. This is also a very helpful guide when you come to renewing the seat. In many cases you will have to remove several layers of top fabric before you reach the original faded fabric. I think that it is rather nice to find under all the different fabrics the one that was originally used. You may prefer to use a fabric and colour of your own choice but think how nice it would be to be able to match the original as closely as possible. Where the fabric has been tucked in you will even be able to see some of the fine colour used perhaps some 80–100 years ago.

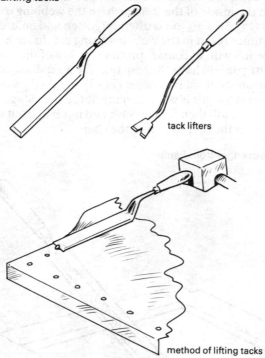

Fig 2 Lifting tacks

tack lifters

method of lifting tacks

When all the outer fabrics are removed the stuffing can be lifted out. You can find quite an assortment of stuffing in chairs, even shredded newspaper which can often make interesting reading. You may find black horsehair or on better-quality chairs, usually older ones, you may come across white horsehair. Coconut fibre and straw are also used. The stuffing in your chair can possibly be used again but take it outside and give it a good beating to remove all the dust and dirt. Horsehair is quite expensive to replace so after you have given it a good clean, tease the fibres out with your fingers and then they can most certainly be used again. After all the fabrics and stuffing have been removed all that remains is the webbing. Lift out the tacks holding the webbing, making a careful note of how the webbing was positioned.

At this stage the chair frame must be checked for any defects and splits which must be repaired before carrying on with the upholstery. When you are satisfied that the frame is sound and free from woodworm, take a rasp or Surform and take off the sharp edges from the inside of the frame where the webbing is going to be fixed (Fig 3). This job is often forgotten and failure to do this can sometimes result in the webbing being cut through. Doing this simple job will, of course, prolong the life of the upholstery. Whilst you still have the rasp out, file a small amount of the wood away on the front two edges (Fig 3) and do the same at the back. The reason for this is when you are at the later stage of fixing the top fabric it will then fold in flush and not bulge out and make it difficult to fit the seat back into the chair.

Fig 3 Removing sharp edges from frame

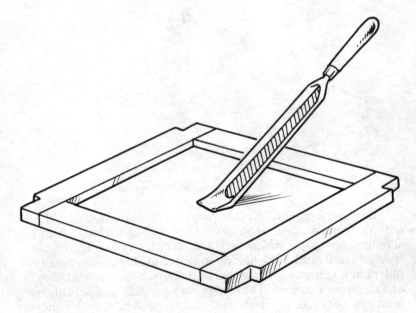

Replacing webbing

Webbing a chair creates no great problems. You will be able to see where the old webbing was fixed so use this as a guide. The size of the tacks required for fixing webbing would be 15 mm (⅝in). Two points worth mentioning are first make sure that each new tack does not go into a hole made by one you have removed, otherwise you may find that it will pull out. Secondly, never drive in the tacks in a straight line as this will tend to split the wood. You must first fold the webbing over about 18 mm (¾ in), and with the fold uppermost put in two tacks (Fig 4); the fold will give the webbing greater strength. Then stagger three more tacks as shown in Fig 5.

Fig 4 Initial securing of webbing

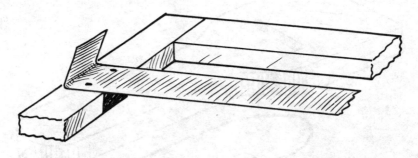

Fig 5 Fully secured webbing

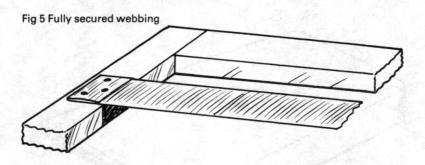

Apart from a pair of scissors and a hammer you will need a webbing stretcher, which is used for pulling the webbing tight. This tool can be easily obtained from a good ironmonger or tool shop and is not too expensive (Fig 6). Should you feel rather mean or have perhaps just one chair to upholster you can make a very simple webbing stretcher from a small piece of scrap wood. You will need a piece of wood 100–125 mm (4–5 in) long, 50 mm (2 in) wide and 25 mm (1 in) thick. Cut a V-shaped slot across one end of the wood and take off any sharp edges with a piece of sandpaper: this makes the tool more comfortable to use (Fig 7).

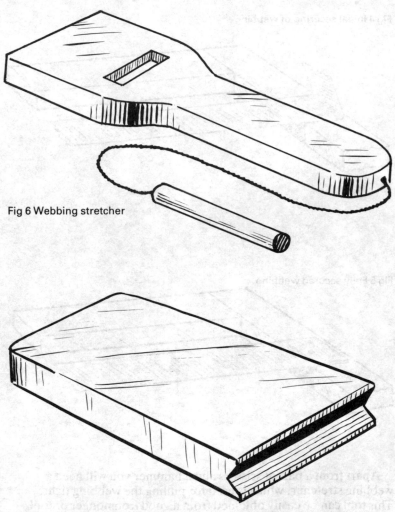

Fig 6 Webbing stretcher

Fig 7 Home-made webbing stretcher

Fig 8 Both types of webbing stretcher in use

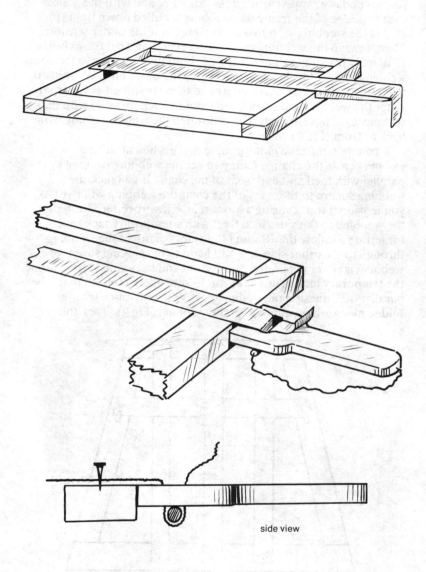

side view

The idea is that after one end of the webbing has been fixed, the surplus end is wrapped around the stretcher and with the V slot over the edge of the frame the webbing is pulled down tight (Fig 8). Fix the webbing with two tacks whilst holding under tension. Then unwrap the webbing from the stretcher and cut off webbing 18 mm (¾ in) longer than the frame. Fold the flap over to the fixed webbing and fix this in the same way as the other end. Webbing is fixed first to the back of the chair and then tensioned at the front. After the webbing has been fixed front to back proceed with the side pieces. These are interlaced through the webbing going from back to front (Fig 9).

A common mistake many people make when attaching the webbing cross the chair is failing to get the webbing running parallel with the front and back of the chair. If you tack the webbing square to the sides of the chair the webbing will twist as you tension it thus causing a loose seat. The procedure for fixing the webbing to the sides is to fix it with a temporary tack, not forgetting to allow the 18 mm (¾ in) fold. Thread the webbing through to the other side and pull hand tight, making sure the webbing is running parallel to the front and back rails. Drive home the temporary tack. Turn over the 18 mm (¾ in) fold so that it is parallel with the side rail of the chair. You will notice that the folded piece is not square with the webbing (Fig 9). Tack the

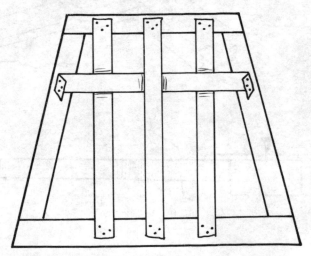

Fig 9 Interlacing webbing showing folded end at sides

webbing down, not forgetting to stagger the tacks. Tension in the same way as already described making absolutely sure the webbing is parallel both to the front and back and there are no twists in the webbing.

Replacing hessian

When the webbing has been fixed it is covered with a piece of hessian or sacking. Cover the whole of the frame and tack around the edges using smaller 9 mm (³⁄₈ in) tacks. This is pulled hand tight. Start from the back by tacking along and pulling tight as you go. When the back has been fixed, stretch the hessian over to the front edge and tack into position. The sides are tacked down in the same way, pulling the hessian tight. Do not fold the hessian around the corners as this will cause a bump when the final fabric is applied and will not allow the seat to fit into the chair properly. Cut the hessian away to form the corners (Fig 10).

Laying stuffing

If you prefer new material for the stuffing this can be obtained from most hobby shops and some large departmental stores. You

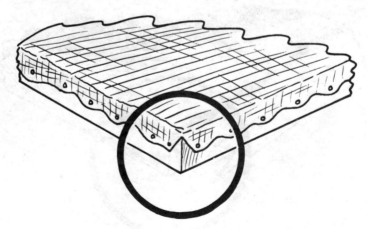

Fig 10 Cutting hessian away to form corner

lay the stuffing on the hessian and start working out from the middle to the edges. This is quite important because if you do not spread the stuffing evenly you will have a very uncomfortable seat. Make sure there is enough stuffing in the centre and also along the edges. When you feel satisfied that it is evenly spread you then cover over the stuffing with calico. This is tacked down in the same way as the hessian but make sure the stuffing is evenly distributed whilst you are doing so.

Replacing decorative fabric

The chair is now ready for its final decorative fabric. The size of your top cover can be taken from the old one you removed. In fact, all the old materials removed from the frame will give you the sizes and amounts of the new materials required. Start fixing the decorative fabric from the back of the chair. Do not fix right up to the corners. Stop about 50 mm (2 in) in from each corner. After having fixed to the back pull and smooth the fabric to the front and tack into position whilst you are fixing the front edge. Smooth out wrinkles as you go, working from the centre outwards. Stop 50 mm (2 in) from the ends. The sides can now be fixed in the same way, removing any creases as you go. Only the corners are then left to be done.

Fig 11 Folding and tucking fabric at corner

These must be done very neatly so as not to spoil all the hard work you have already done. Fold the material on the back rail around to the sides making very neat folds. Cut away any surplus material that will make the corner look bulky. Having satisfied yourself it is neat enough, tack into place pulling tightly and removing any creases. The side piece of fabric is then folded and tucked in carefully (Fig 11) and fixed with tacks to make a neat and tidy job. Repeat this process on the other corners on the back of the chair. The front of the chair is done in exactly the same way except that the sides are folded round the front first then the front edge of the fabric is brought over the front edge so that when you look at the finished chair you do not see any unsightly folds. This part of the operation needs patience and care. Corners are not easy so it is best to practise on a scrap of wood, suitably padded, to represent the corner of a chair. When you feel capable of doing a good job start on the real thing.

Finally all that remains to be done is to tack a piece of hessian to the underside of the chair to keep out any dust. Fold the hessian under, before you tack it down, to make a neat and tidy job.

Do not forget that the many hundreds of night classes being held up and down the country are there to help you, not only giving you a social evening but also a means to learn to do something well worthwhile. I have only described how to re-upholster a simple drop-in seat and there are, of course, chairs with springs, chairs with buttons, pleated chairs and so on. A five-year apprenticeship is required for a professional upholsterer to learn the trade and even then throughout the rest of his life he learns new things every day. So do not be too disappointed if your upholstery is not too good. You will achieve better results the more you do, so start by practising on simple projects and work your way up as you gain more experience.

Useful tips

Some useful tips I have learnt from professional upholsterers are as follows.
1   The old springs taken from worn-out chairs make very useful cramps. A normal spring will make about four cramps. Cut the spring with a hacksaw. Bend the cramps to shape (Fig 12) and you

will find them more than useful when you are trying to hold small pieces of wood, for example, whilst the glue sets.

2 If a chair has decorative brass studs around the seat these can be reused if they are taken out carefully. As you remove each stud, place it in a piece of card or a polystyrene tile in the order in which

Fig 12 Old spring cut to produce C-shaped cramps

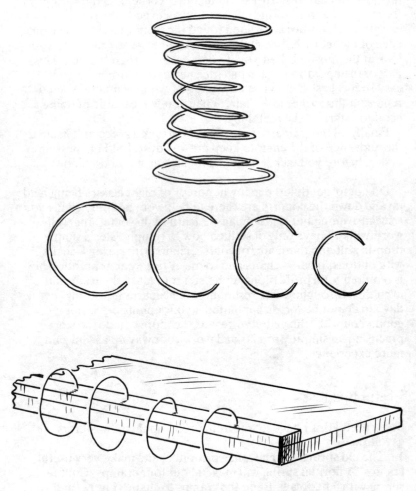

it came out. These are put back in the same order when the upholstery has been completed. The reason for this is that the studs are shiny near the front edge due to people sliding on and off the chair but around the sides they will be rather dull and it does look rather odd if they have been jumbled up and put back with shiny ones alternating with dull ones. Attention to a small point like this adds that touch of professionalism to the completed work.

3   If you need to buy some horsehair for a chair or settee you are reupholstering it is best to search around for an old horsehair mattress. These can be picked up for a few pounds at auctions and will make you a great saving against buying new horsehair.

Repairs to China

Old china suffers from nearly all the problems that furniture does as over years of wear parts become broken off, chipped and cracked. I would not suggest major repairs to dining plates or cups because, in agreement with some schools of thought, I would deem this unhygienic. There are, however, odd pieces of decorative china — such as vases, figures or jardinières — that are quite suitable for repair and, after all, each of us has probably at some time stuck back a handle on a cup. Broken pieces of china can be bought quite cheaply at auctions or from antique shops, all you have to do then is to repair them. I suggest looking first in the cupboard for a broken cup or plate to practise on. But I must emphasise here once again that if you are unsure that the item you have bought or inherited is of great value then you must have it authenticated, because even a badly damaged item of china could be of great historical and monetary value and any amateur attempt at restoring it may destroy any such value.

Gluing two pieces together

Firstly, you will almost certainly find some china that has already been stuck together and repaired badly. You will, of course, have to undo all this work. Most glues can be softened by immersing the whole item in water and leaving it perhaps for 24 hours until the glue has softened enough for you to separate the pieces. Place the item in a plastic bowl or bucket as you are less liable to do any

Fig 1 Securing join with self-adhesive plastic tape while glue sets

further damage to the item by knocking it against a tap or the hard edge of a sink. A piece of sponge laid in the bottom first will also give more protection. Use cold water unless the glue is stubborn. If this is the case then warm water can be added. Never immerse a piece of china directly into hot water as this may cause the china to expand, thus making the damage worse than when you started.

Test the item at intervals to see if the glue has softened enough to allow the pieces to be pulled apart. When the pieces eventually do come apart leave them to soak until all the glue can be removed from the surface of the break. Any particles left on the two surfaces will not allow the join to close together. Small particles of glue can be removed with the aid of a needle. Fit the two pieces together and when every trace of glue is removed you should be able to see no more than a hair-line crack.

At this stage the pieces are ready for gluing together. They must, of course, be left to dry thoroughly. I find the most useful glue for sticking china is the epoxy type where there are two packs, one containing the glue and the other the hardener. These are mixed together in equal proportions to become active. Nearly all glues tend to yellow with age so add just a sprinkle of white pigment, titanium dioxide (available from artists' suppliers), and thoroughly mix with the glue. Of course, if the piece you are working on is, say, dark blue than add a powdered blue dye to the glue. When using epoxy glue do so in a warm room because if the glue is cold it tends to be rather thick and you will be unable to join the pieces of china closely together. Squeeze just enough glue onto the two surfaces for them to be joined, any excess glue will have to be cleaned off.

The two pieces will then have to be held in place whilst the glue sets. Sellotape is one good idea but it is not particularly elastic and can be difficult to apply. Some people swear by brown sticky paper, because in theory as the paper dries out it shrinks and cramps the join very tightly. My favourite is self-adhesive plastic electrician's tape as this can be pulled rather tight. Since it is also very flexible it is ideal for all the difficult contours you are likely to find when repairing china (Fig 1). Because of this variety of shapes and the difficulty in holding many of them, Plasticine makes a very good mould in which the piece of china can be held in any position for you to work on it (Fig 2).

Fig 2 China vase in Plasticine mould ready to be worked on

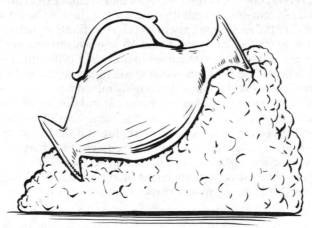

Filling gaps or chips

This can be done quite easily using an epoxy putty which is similar to the glue except that it comes in two solid pieces. Equal lengths are cut from the blocks and kneaded together until the colour is even.

Coloured pigments can be added to match the surrounding colour of the chip you are going to replace. This is done to form an undercoat of colour. With the colour completely mixed in with the putty it is ready for use.

I always apply a spot of epoxy glue to the edges of the parts about to be filled. This gives a better bond to the epoxy putty which is then spread or moulded into place. Leave the putty just proud of the surface and smooth down to the edges by dipping your fingers in water and working the putty to a smooth finish. You can use an old modelling knife dipped in water in the same way. Do not leave the putty too proud of the surface as this has to be filed smooth when it has hardened.

After leaving the putty to harden and dry for approximately 24 hours, you now have to rub it down to the level of the surrounding china taking great care not to scratch the glaze. Use glasspaper No. 000 on the final stages. A small piece on the end of your finger is sufficient. Finish off with a flour paper so that the surface feels as smooth as the surrounding area.

All that remains now is that the piece of epoxy putty has to be painted to match exactly the colour of the piece of china. There are several ways of doing this. Many of them require heat and nearly all of them are difficult if you are not skilled in the art of painting. Try the following easy method. Add finely ground dyes like Dylon to an absolutely clear varnish or polyurethene until you have the exact colour. Dylon comes in dozens of different colours so there is no excuse for a mismatch if you take your time. With the correct colour and the dye thoroughly mixed with the varnish apply this to the segment of putty, being careful not to get any on the existing china. Always use a very fine sable brush for this job; it is no good expecting to achieve a perfect finish if the brush you use is of poor quality. Several coats may be required to achieve the correct colour and eight hours must be allowed for each coat to dry completely. After several coats you should find that you have a perfect finish and only you will know about the gaps or chips.

Safety with chemicals

During the course of restoring old furniture you will use several different types of chemicals. All liquid chemicals need to be handled very carefully.

1   Make sure that each bottle or container is correctly labelled, that the lid or stopper is in place and that it is stored according to the manufacturer's instructions.

2   Proper ventilation is essential for many of the products you will use, so keep a window open to allow any toxic fumes to escape.

3   Do not smoke whilst using flammable materials and dispose of any old rags that have been saturated with flammable liquids.

4   Wear the proper safety equipment — protective glasses, rubber gloves and an apron.

5   Be very careful when opening lids as some chemicals may build up slight pressure and splash up as the lid is removed.

6   Keep a properly equipped first-aid box handy for minor cuts and grazes.

7   Always add acids to water and never water to acids.

Further copies of this book are available from:
As Good As New
PO Box 50
Market Harborough
Leicestershire

Cheques/PO's made payable to ITV Books
price £1.50 (which includes post and packing)

List of suppliers

Wood veneers,
tools, mouldings
and polishes

World of Wood Ltd
2 Industrial Estate
Mildenhall
Suffolk
(catalogue available)

Tools

Stanley Tools Ltd
Woodside
Sheffield
(catalogue available)

Reproduction brass handles
and fittings

John Harwood & Co
28 Fairfields
Bromley Cross
Bolton BL7 9EE
(catalogue available)

Polishes, wire wool,
strippers, glasspaper,
powdered dyes, bees-wax

W S Jenkins & Co Ltd
Jeco Works
Tariff Road
London N17 0EN
(catalogue available)

All upholstery requirements

The Russell Trading Co
75 Paradise Street
Liverpool
(catalogue available)

With the exception of Stanley Tools all these companies will
supply direct by mail. Other chemicals can be obtained from your
local chemist in small quantities.

Also In This Series

Home-made For The Home (Book 2) This fully illustrated book gives many ideas and clear step by step instructions on how to use a variety of skills and crafts to enable you to make attractive and useful articles for the home, in the home. £1

Home and Design Written by expert designer and author, Mary Gilliatt, this book offers excellent advice, hints and practical aids covering all aspects of home design. Packed with illustrations and black and white photographs. £1

Learn To Sing This helpful book, written by writer, singer and teacher Graham Hewitt, provides a wealth of practical advice to help improve your singing ability and general vocal skills. £1

Doctor Dr Ken Dickinson, TV medical consultant and University Medical Officer, has written this excellent book to cover such topics as Asthma, Blood Disorders and Arthritis to help you better understand the workings of the body, what can go wrong and available treatment. **£1**

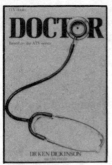

Vet Practical advice for all caring pet-owners is provided in this fully illustrated book written by vet, John Speer. From dogs to ponies, cats to budgerigars, Vet contains a mass of information on selection, handling and care of most household pets. **£1.50**

Each or all of these books are available at the stated price (which includes post and packing) from:

ITV Books
P O Box 50
Market Harborough
Leicestershire
Cheques/P O's made payable to ITV Books
(Please state clearly which books are requested)